AN INTRODUCTION TO

NAUTICAL SCIENCE

AN INTRODUCTION TO

NAUTICAL SCIENCE

CARL CHASE

W.W. NORTON & COMPANY

NEW YORK

LONDON

Printed in the United States of America
Excerpt(s) from *Heat Engines* by John F. Sandfort, copyright © 1962 by
Educational Services, Inc. Used by permission of Doubleday, a division of
Bantam, Doubleday, Dell Publishing Group, Inc.

The text of this book is composed in Sabon,
with the display set in Sabon.
Composition by The Sarabande Press.
Book design by The Sarabande Press.

First Edition
Library of Congress Cataloging-in-Publication Data

Chase, Carl.
An introduction to nautical science/Carl Chase.
p. cm.
Includes bibliographical references.
1. Seamanship. 2. Navigation. I. Title.
VK541.C48 1991
623.8—dc20   90-37998

ISBN 0-393-02850-X
W.W. Norton & Company, Inc., 500 Fifth Avenue, New York, N.Y. 10110
W.W. Norton & Company, Ltd., 10 Coptic Street, London WC1A 1PU
1   2   3   4   5   6   7   8   9   0

CONTENTS

PREFACE

When I wrote it in 1987, this book was intended to provide the framework for an intensive six-week course preparing students for going to sea in a modern sailing vessel. It is the result of my having developed such a course for the Sea Education Association of Woods Hole, Massachusetts, for the "shore component" of their Sea Semester program. In this program, college students, some with and many without any previous experience in boats, first spend six weeks "on campus" in Woods Hole, then go to sea for six weeks on a 100-foot schooner to put into practice what they have learned.

Due to the very limited amount of time available, one of the main objectives of the course as it evolved was to identify just what was most important for the about-to-be sailor to know when the lines were let go and he found himself part of the crew with real responsibilities toward the operation of the ship. Next it was necessary to discover to what *depth* it was appropriate to teach the various subjects, and finally it was vital that the presentation of the material be well grounded in common sense. Good seamanship is after all simply the application of good common sense to nautical situations, and if that attitude could be conveyed in the classroom, then whatever was skipped or missed there could be figured out at sea!

Therefore what we have in this book is by no means a thorough coverage of any of its topics, but rather a distilled explanation of each; from its underlying principles to its practical, shipboard applications. For the land-locked student, any chapter could serve as an introduction to a great deal of further reading and study. The exciting assumption, however, is that the book-learning will be followed by the experience of going to sea, where all the lessons become seen, heard, and felt.

ACKNOWLEDGMENTS

The writing of this book is the direct result of my work with the Sea Education Association from 1980 to 1987. I owe a large debt of gratitude to Dr. James F. Millinger, then dean and acting executive director of S.E.A., for his encouragement and enthusiasm for my experiments and ideas in shaping the Nautical Science course. Thank you, Jim, for your confidence!

As I prepared to leave S.E.A. and proposed writing this book to leave as a text for the course, it was Dr. Susan E. Humphries, currently dean of S.E.A., who backed the idea and got the first edition into print. Many thanks to you, Susan, for that help and encouragement along the way!

Of course the bottom line is the students, and my biggest debt is to them for their unending patience and perseverance in teaching me how to teach! Thanks to you all.

Carl A. Chase

Brooksville, Maine
August 1989

INTRODUCTION

To travel across the water in a vessel propelled by the wind will always challenge man's ingenuity. Expanding technologies and available energy resources may render it more or less practical, but the fascination will always be there. Why? Because as long as the air moves over the water there is free energy there at the interface for anyone to use, and the technology needed to harness it is simple, visible, tangible—available to anyone with common sense and the desire to reach for it. With no more than a wooden shingle, a sheet of paper, and some string, a prototype energy converter can be built which will demonstrate how to use it.

To sail *far* across an ocean in sufficient comfort and safety to be able to accomplish a mission—be it the carrying of passengers or cargo, the collecting of data or the harvesting of fish—calls for more sophistication, but since the sailboat at sea has no other resources than the wind, the water, and whatever she may have brought with her in the way of fuel, food, spare parts, and human ingenuity, there is good reason to keep the technology as simple as possible.

This book is intended to give you who are interested in going to sea in a sailing vessel some framework upon which to build your understanding of how one works. The real understanding will come with the voyage, when the forces, causes, and effects discussed here are actually seen and felt. If you are already an experienced sailor you will have the advantage of being able to relate what you read here to past experience. Discovering the theory behind things you have done or seen done will give them new significance. If you have never sailed you will find the concepts are amply illustrated with references to other aspects of common experience.

In each topic we will move quickly from general theory to specific applications of that theory to the boat, and from there to how you as crew members figure in the process of making her sail and fulfill her mission at sea.

AN INTRODUCTION TO

NAUTICAL SCIENCE

CHAPTER ONE

Basic Physics

L ook at the boat from the dock. Look at a model of the boat, or a good photograph. She is complex-looking: spars, rigging, sails, deck structures, hatches, rails, hull, machinery, fittings, blocks, and hundreds of things as yet without names. For the moment overlook the complexity. Step back farther and remember that first and foremost the boat is a physical object—a thing—subject to all the laws of physics. It will help us to understand the boat if we refresh our familiarity with some of these basic concepts.

She has weight—that is, *gravity* pulls her downward. She floats— that is, something holds her up in the water against gravity. Being a mass and having weight means that she also has *inertia*—that tendency of things to stay as they are, either at rest or in motion. Give her a push and she will respond by pushing back. It takes a force to get her moving and another one just as big to stop her again.

Since we will be talking about the boat as a single object it will simplify matters if we remember that any object has a theoretical center of its mass known as its *center of gravity*. Gravity acts on everything, but instead of trying to picture its pull on each and every part of the object, we can sum up all these small forces and picture them as one single force acting at the center of gravity of the object.

For a regularly shaped object of uniform density such as a brick, the center of gravity is easily imagined at the geometric center of the brick. In the case of the boat the location of the center of gravity is not so obvious. She is not of regular shape, nor uniformly dense. Her mass is comprised of all the bits and pieces of her construction, equipment, supplies, and crew. Moreover, some of these are free to move about. With full tanks and the crew on deck preparing to get underway her center of gravity is in one spot. Three weeks later with fresh water used up and the crew all aloft looking for land, it is somewhere else!

The knowledge of where a boat's center of gravity will be when she is built is an extremely important part of designing a boat. Without it one could not predict how the boat will behave in the water, whether she will stay upright, or sail, or be safe and comfortable to live aboard. The task of calculating it is tedious, and boils down to accounting for the position and weight of every possible thing that will be on the boat. Once the boat is built, launched, and outfitted, the true center of gravity can be located by experiment. Hopefully, it will not be far from the architect's prediction.

Knowing the location of the boat's center of gravity enables us to represent her weight (the force of gravity) by a *vector*. A vector used to represent a force is drawn as an arrow, and shows us two things: its length shows the size of the force, and its direction shows the direction in which the force is pushing or pulling. In the case of the force of gravity, of course, this will always be vertically downward (Figure 1-1).

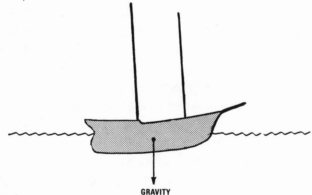

GRAVITY

FIG. 1-1

When we see an object being acted on by a force, we reasonably expect the object to respond, and the response we expect is that it will *accelerate in the direction the force is acting.* With no more information than that shown in Figure 1-1 we would expect to see the boat accelerating downward in response to the force of gravity. The fact that this (usually) does not happen is, of course, due to the other force which is (usually) present and opposing the force of gravity: the force of *buoyancy.* Remember Archimedes in the bathtub? Where does this force come from? It must be considerable because it supports 100,000-ton supertankers as well as a five-ton yacht, as well as a rowboat or Styrofoam cup.

Buoyancy is just another manifestation of the force of gravity. In a bowl of water the surface is flat and level. Any water that might have stuck up has been pulled down by gravity; any holes or valleys have been filled in—gravity has that water as far down as it can go. Now if we make a hole in the water by pushing some of it aside we are working against gravity, and it will try to pull the displaced water back into the hole. That means that water is pushing back upward against whatever has pushed it aside. The strength of this upward push will equal the weight of the water that was pushed aside.

This is true on any scale. When a boat is placed in the ocean it displaces water, the sea surface rises, and gravity tries to pull it back resulting in an upward force on the boat. Since seawater weighs 64 pounds per cubic foot, every cubic foot that is displaced results in a 64 pound force of buoyancy.

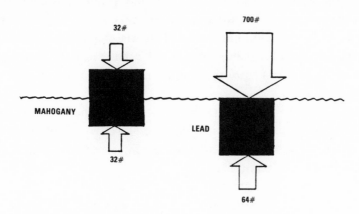

FIG. 1-2

A cubic foot of lead weighs about 700 pounds and a cubic foot of mahogany about 32 pounds. Let gravity pull each one downward into the sea (Figure 1-2). As they sink deeper into the water, more and more water is displaced and the force of buoyancy increases. When the lead is totally submerged it has displaced 1 cubic foot so the force of buoyancy has reached a maximum of 64 pounds. Since the force of gravity is 700 pounds, however, the lead sinks. The mahogany, on the other hand, is only half submerged when the force of buoyancy equals its weight: 32 pounds. The forces of gravity and buoyancy are equal and added together leave no unbalanced forces acting on the block so it floats where it is neither sinking nor rising. Notice that if by some means it were made to go deeper into the water, it would displace more and the force of buoyancy would then exceed its weight. This would make a net upward force which would cause the block to accelerate upward— until it once again displaced exactly 32 pounds of water.

When all the forces acting on an object are balanced (i.e.: equal and opposite) the object is said to be in *equilibrium*. The floating block of mahogany reaches equilibrium when it is half-submerged and the force of gravity and force of buoyancy are equal. A car sitting in the parking lot is in equilibrium. The force of gravity is matched by an upward force from the pavement and there are no other forces acting on the car. But start the engine and put it in "drive" and we have a new force pushing it forward. The car is no longer in equilibrium; the forces on it are unbalanced, and predictably it accelerates. Assuming the push from the engine continues the same size, what will happen? The car will accelerate to some speed and (assuming also a smooth, level road) then steady out at that speed.

Or tow a model boat in a tank by a string attached to a falling weight. At first the weight is an unbalanced force which accelerates the boat through the water, but at some point its speed will steady out—no more acceleration.

In both cases a new state of equilibrium has been reached. As speed increased in response to the propelling force, a new force appeared and began to affect each vehicle. The instant it began to move forward the car felt frictional *resistance* to its movement (the tires on the road, its mechanical parts moving together, etc.) and wind resistance as it pushed through the air. The boat also felt some resistance from the air, but more from the water, a heavier fluid to push through. These resistance forces were directly opposed to the propelling forces. Their size was a function of the vehicle's speed, so as it accelerated the resistance grew until it became as big as the propelling force (Figure 1-3).

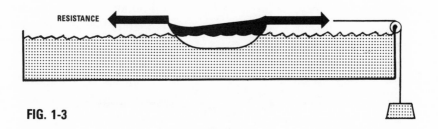

FIG. 1-3

Now once more we see that there are no unbalanced forces at work. This does not mean that the vehicle stops, but only that no further acceleration happens. The vehicle will remain in motion *at a constant speed and steady direction* as long as the forces stay balanced. It is again in equilibrium.

To pursue the example of the boat a bit further, imagine what would happen to its state of equilibrium if it were to sail into a patch of molasses. Suddenly the resistance force would become much larger and overbalance the propelling force. Now with a net force *against* it, the boat would lose speed. But remember that resistance, being a function of speed, will decrease as speed decreases. The boat will slow down until the resistance again matches the propelling force. Of course, if we did not want the boat to lose speed, and had seen the molasses coming, we could have added weight to the string so that the propelling force increased as much as the resistance did, thereby maintaining equilibrium without losing speed.

Sailing a boat is largely a matter of maintaining equilibrium among many forces acting on the hull and sails. It is important to have a clear sense of what equilibrium means and does not mean before going on to a more specific discussion of sailing.

We have used vectors already and will be using them a great deal more because they are graphic and make visualizing a situation easier. We have seen how the effect of forces acting either together or directly opposite each other can be readily assessed by simple addition or subtraction of the lengths of vectors. The sailboat is constantly affected by many forces acting in many *different* directions, however, and we will want to combine and simplify them into one total force also.

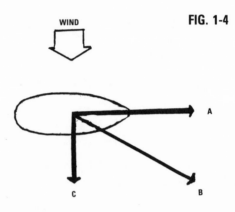

WIND

FIG. 1-4

A

C

B

In Figure 1-4 our model boat is being accelerated by the weight and string (vector A) as before, but now there is also a crosswind (vector B) exerting a sideways force on it. Either one of those forces alone would result in the boat accelerating in that particular direction at the rate shown by the vector's length. Acting together, however, they have a combined effect shown by vector C. Since we are not concerned with numbers and accuracy of scale, we can graphically combine vector A and vector B by sketching a parallelogram with them as two sides. Vector C, their *resultant,* is the diagonal of the parallelogram.

One of the most appealing aspects of sailing as a means of propulsion is that the energy doing the work of moving the boat is free—at least as far as we are concerned. Of course this "free" energy which drives the boat arrived on the earth as solar radiation. However, to use this energy to move the boat, and to keep ourselves safe and healthy and comfortable on her, and to accomplish the task we go to sea to do requires additional sources of energy.

At sea we will have available two sources of energy other than the wind—at least we will have them until they are used up. They are *food* and *diesel fuel*. The energy converting devices that will use this energy to do the needed work are ourselves and diesel engines. The engine will be looked at in detail in Chapter Five, and how our body converts food into a 100-pound pull on a halyard is a matter for another course. What is relevant here, however, is how we are able to change that 100-pound pull into a force great enough to raise a 400-pound sail, or control the other huge forces developed by a large sailing vessel. Some very basic and simple mechanical principles are put to great use on the boat to multiply our strength through the concept of *mechanical advantage*.

Most of the work of sailing a boat (setting sails, trimming sheets, steering) involves moving large weights or overcoming large forces. Many of these tasks are too big for a person to confront directly. The average person cannot lift 400 pounds by hand, but with the help of a crowbar it could be done relatively easily. Crowbars are not commonly used in sailing, but the principle of the *lever* is found all over the boat, in the rigging, on deck, in the engine room, and even in the galley.

To review the principle of the lever, first remember that what we are interested in is doing *work* and the effort required to do it. By the definition used in mechanics, work is done when a force moves an object. One could strain at that 400-pound weight for half a hour and end up exhausted but, if it did not move, no work would have been done. If four people get together and lift it three feet off the ground, then work *is* done. The amount done is 1200 foot-pounds, or the weight of the object times the distance it was moved. Together the four people exert 1200 foot-pounds of effort to accomplish 1200 foot-pounds of work. In terms of forces and distances over which they act, this can be stated thus:

$$\text{Effort} \times \text{Effort Distance} = \text{Resistance} \times \text{Resistance Distance}$$

So if we are to lift a 400-pound weight three feet we will have to deliver 1200 foot-pounds of effort *one way or another*. And there is the key that makes all things possible ("Give me a fulcrum and a

21

long enough lever and I will move the earth," said Archimedes). We can arrange for many combinations of effort and effort distance to make 1200 foot-pounds, and the lever is one means of doing this (Figure 1-5).

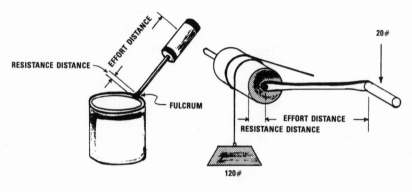

FIG. 1-5   **FIG. 1-6**

There are endless examples of the lever principle at work ashore as well as at sea. Take a second look the next time you pry the lid off a paint can, or the top off a beer bottle. To analyze the situation, first locate the fulcrum or pivot point. Then identify the resistance point and see how far it is from the fulcrum (resistance distance). Compare that distance to the distance between the fulcrum and where you apply the effort (effort distance). The ratio of these distances tells you the *mechanical advantage* that the lever gives you. The *amounts* of effort and resistance will be in the opposite ratio.

$$E \text{ dist} / R \text{ dist} = \text{Mechanical Advantage} = R / E$$

The lever principle does not always look like a crowbar or church key. The crank on a winch (Figure 1-6) is a lever that works continuously around a pivot point. The longer the handle and the smaller the drum, the greater will be the mechanical advantage. The winch shown would give a mechanical advantage of 6:1, so with a mere 20-pound effort we could lift 120 pounds. The inescapable trade-off, however, is that we must move the handle six times as far as the weight moves. A mechanical advantage does not do the job for us, it just makes it possible!

On a sailing vessel the rigging is full of *blocks* (Figure 1-7). The rigging is there to support and manage the spars and sails, which are heavy in themselves, and under terrific strain when full of wind, and the block and tackle is what enables us to handle those forces safely and easily. Once again it is the lever in disguise.

To set a sail, one corner of it must be hoisted up to the top of the mast. Without a block this would require that someone go aloft and pull the sail up—neither safe nor easy. With a single block at the masthead, however, the sail can be raised by pulling down on its *halyard* from the deck. It will require a pull equal to the weight of the sail, plus a little for friction. This can be understood if we picture the *sheave* of the block as being a continuous lever with its fulcrum at the axle or pin. The resistance (the sail) and the effort (our pull) are equidistant from the fulcrum so they must be equal in size also. A block used in this way is a convenience, but does not offer a mechanical advantage.

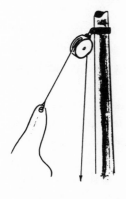
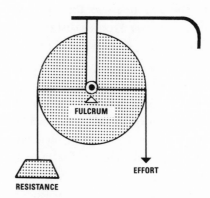

FIG. 1-7

The same block can be rigged in another way which can make the job of hoisting very large weights relatively easy. This time (Figure 1-8) one end of the halyard is made fast at the top of the mast, and the block is attached to the head of the sail. The question now is, if we were to go up the mast and pull the other end of the halyard, how much force would be needed?

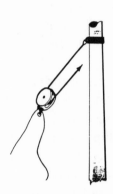

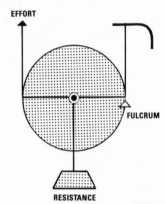

FIG. 1-8

The correct answer is only half as much force as before. To understand why, again picture the block as a lever. Identify the fulcrum, resistance distance, and effort distance. In this case the lever has been rearranged. The fulcrum or pivot point is now at one end. The resistance is hanging from the middle (pin) and the effort is being applied at the other end. Therefore the ratio of effort distance to resistance distance is 2:1. If the sail weighs 100 pounds we can raise it with a pull of 50—but must pull twice as much line as it goes up.

At this point we would fetch another block to secure at the masthead so that we could go back down on deck and pull more comfortably. In fact we could fetch several more blocks and begin doubling or tripling up on what we have. We will find that every time we add another block to the load, we increase the mechanical advantage by two—in theory, anyway—but we also add friction so the true gain is somewhat less. Some of the more common tackles are shown in Figure 1-9. Study them and see why they have the mechanical advantage that they do.

The same relationships between resistance, effort, and the relative distances they move hold true for the other basic machine: the *inclined plane* or ramp. This is another fundamental way to gain a mechanical advantage and overcome a large force with a smaller

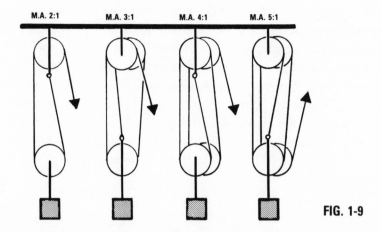

FIG. 1-9

one. In Figure 1-10 the 400-pound weight is being raised three feet off the ground by a 40-pound push using a ramp. As before, the mechanical advantage is the ratio of effort distance to resistance distance, and like the lever, the inclined plane appears most commonly in slightly disguised forms.

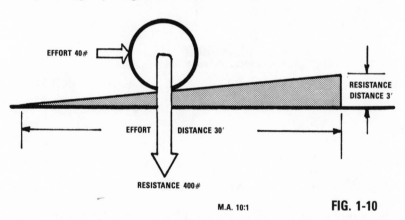

M.A. 10:1   FIG. 1-10

Wedges around the mast at deck level are easily tapped down and thus exert a great sideways force against the mast, holding it securely. Another very common example of the inclined plane principle is the screw, and all its relatives: bolts, clamps, turnbuckles, etc. A thread cut into a rod is in fact a ramp wrapped around the rod. The nut with matching thread rides up and down the rod as it is rotated. To analyze the situation pictured by the clamp (Figure

1-11) we again ask how far does the effort have to move in order to move the resistance a given amount? If the "pitch" of the thread shown is 10 threads per inch, we know the clamp will close ⅒-inch for every rotation of the handle. If the effort is applied at the end of the handle and moves through 20 inches in one rotation, we have a ratio of E dist. to R dist. of 20 to ⅒. Therefore the mechanical advantage of the clamp is 200:1, and a five-pound effort on the handle will produce a 1000-pound squeeze! Finer thread and a longer handle would make this even more impressive.

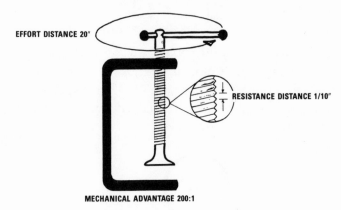

FIG. 1-11

SUMMARY

The apparent complexity of the sailboat yields very easily to the most basic physical concepts. The rigging is a study in mechanical advantage, the hull floats according to the laws of buoyancy, and moves according to the laws of motion in response to forces from the wind and water. Even the diesel engine, once dissected, loses its bewildering aspect. In fact, there is relatively little on the modern sailing vessel that Archimedes, Newton, Bernoulli, and Boyle would be at a loss to explain.

Until you are on board, *feeling* the forces at work, *seeing* their cause and effect, the hardest part will be visualizing how things work. But the concepts, laws, and principles are all easily demonstrated in simple ways, and should be whenever possible, for if a picture is worth 1,000 words, a demonstration is worth a large book.

CHAPTER TWO

Stability

The term *stability* refers to a vessel's tendency to stay upright in the water. This tendency may be strong or weak, or, under certain conditions, may appear in reverse as a tendency to capsize. Intuition might suggest that since we do not want the boat tipping over, more is always better where stability is concerned. But this is not necessarily the case because stability is usually achieved only at the expense of some other qualities as important to the success of the boat as staying upright. For the naval architect the stability question usually involves judicious compromise to produce a boat which will fulfill her purpose safely and efficiently.

It is entirely possible for a boat to have too much stability. While this might mean that she'd never tip over or heel more than a certain amount, it would also likely mean that her motion at sea would be uncomfortable, dangerous, or even self-destructive. The forces that work to right a boat arise in response to forces that are trying to heel her over. They are engaged in a continual contest whenever the boat is afloat. The boat and her crew must be strong enough to withstand the wear and tear that results. A boat with too much stability may fight back so vigorously that she throws people overboard or does damage to herself, whereas one with somewhat less stability would find her way more gently through the same conditions.

The forces trying to upset the boat are many. Some are forces of nature such as wind, waves, or ice freezing in the rigging. Others are the results of actions of the master and crew handling and loading the boat. The countering force which causes the boat to right herself comes about through the interaction of the force of gravity pulling the boat down, and the force of buoyancy pushing the boat up. For convenience, all the weight of the boat is considered to act downward at her center of gravity (G), and all the buoyant force of the water to act upward at her center of buoyancy (B). We already know that these opposing forces are of equal size for a boat that is floating. If they were unequal the boat would either sink or rise in the water. The question of concern now is whether or not they are directly opposed, that is, vertically in line.

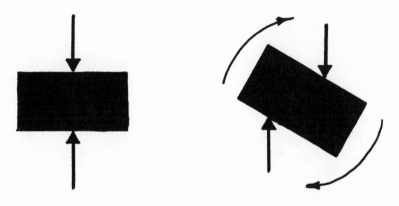

FIG. 2-1

If you push with equal force on opposite sides of a brick, and are careful to align your fingers directly opposite each other, nothing moves (Figure 2-1), but if you offset your fingers by the least amount the brick will rotate in response to the forces.

In a boat, G and B may or may not be vertically aligned at any moment, thus the forces of gravity and buoyancy may or may not be directly opposed. At any time when they are *not*, there exists a tendency for the boat to rotate, and it is usual to picture the rotation as taking place around G as a center (Figure 2-2). If G is taken as the pivot point, then the strength of the tendency to rotate is a function of the upward force of buoyancy (which is equal in size to the force of gravity—and therefore the weight of the boat) and the amount of *horizontal* distance between G and B. This distance is called the

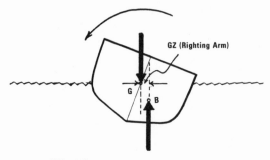

FIG. 2-2

righting arm (GZ). An increase in either the force of buoyancy or in the length of the righting arm will produce a stronger tendency to rotate and vice versa.

Figure 2-3 shows a log floating in the water. It is symmetrically shaped and of even density throughout. Intuition tells us that it will not remain in position A, but will come to rest in position B. How can we explain this in terms of forces which will rotate the log from position A to position B and then keep it there?

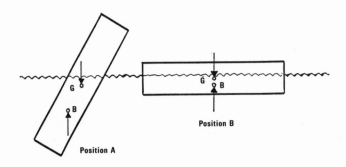

FIG. 2-3

It is first necessary to locate the center of gravity and center of buoyancy of the log. Since the log is uniform, G is located at its geometric center, and will always be there no matter how the log is oriented. B, the center of buoyancy, is defined as the center of the *submerged portion* of the log. In position A this is an irregular shape whose geometric center is not obvious, but there are ways of

finding it. Computation would be most accurate but is very complicated for complex shapes. A fairly accurate result can be obtained
by cutting the shape out of paper, and balancing it on a sharp point.
In position B the location of point B is again obvious.

The vectors in Figure 2-3 represent the force of gravity acting
downward at G, and the force of buoyancy acting upward at B. It
should be apparent in position A that a rotating tendency is present
due to the horizontal offset of G and B, whereas in position B there
is no rotating tendency because G and B are vertically aligned.
What happens between positions A and B?

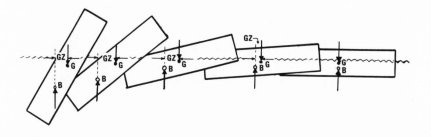

FIG. 2-4

Since B is always at the center of the submerged portion, it must
respond to any change in that portion's shape. In this case as the log
rotates B gradually shifts, first to the left, then to the right (Figure
2-4). As it moves, what happens to the log's tendency to rotate?

Remember that the strength of the rotating tendency (called the
righting moment) is the product of the force of buoyancy and GZ,
the righting arm. There is no change in the force of buoyancy since
the weight of the log does not change, but GZ, the horizontal
distance between G and B, *does* change as B shifts. Thus we find the
righting moment first getting bigger, then smaller and smaller, and
finally disappearing altogether as GZ becomes zero. With a GZ of
zero, the force of buoyancy, though still present, produces no rotating effect of the log. Until some external force again tilts the log
from this position of equilibrium, there is no righting moment. The
instant it is disturbed, however, its underwater shape changes, B

shifts in response, creating a GZ, and there is righting moment working to bring the log level again.

With respect to this side view, we can say that the log is *stable* because it will tend to return to its original position whenever it is disturbed by a outside force. Looking at the log end-on, however, is a different matter.

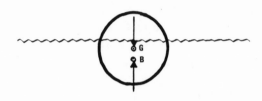

FIG. 2-5

G is still at the center of the log, and B at the center of the submerged portion. They are vertically aligned, so the log is at rest. If an external force rolls the log one way or the other, what happens?

Nothing happens, because the shape of the submerged portion does not change; the log simply comes to rest in the new position. It is equally content to float any way up in the water, and is said to have *neutral stability,* a quality not generally desirable in a boat!

From this it should be clear that the underwater shape of a boat has a great deal to do with her stability characteristics. Consider two sailboats of identical displacement (weight) and rig, but of different hull shape.

In response to a 20-knot breeze, the one that is wide and shallow will heel over less far than the one that is narrow and deep. They must both generate the same righting moment to counter the force of the wind on the rig, and since the force of buoyancy is the same for both, this means that they must make the same righting arm. As can be seen in Figure 2-6, the wide boat produces this righting arm at a 10° heel angle, while the narrow boat must heel to 20° before B shifts that far. The wide boat would be characterized as being *stiff,* and the narrow boat as being *tender.* There is nothing inherently good or bad about a boat's being stiff or tender, it is just one aspect of the stability question that has to be considered with others. For

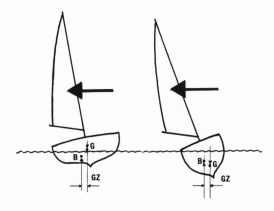

FIG. 2-6

example, saying that a boat is stiff is really saying that she produces a large righting arm at low angles of heel. This means that she will have a quick and vigorous response to being heeled or rolled. For a large ship in a seaway this could be a dangerous characteristic. For a small vessel in protected waters it might not be a problem, and for still other types of craft—a barge, perhaps—it might be just what is needed to keep her as level as possible.

In designing a new boat, or in evaluating the stability of an existing one, there are two main considerations: *initial stability,* and *range of stability.* Initial stability refers to the nature of the boat's response to being heeled slightly, whereas her range of stability tells us how far she can heel without capsizing or filling with water. Both can be shown on a graph called a *righting arm curve,* where the angle of heel is plotted against the length of the righting arm that is produced at that angle.

Figure 2-7 shows in cross section a boat heeling progressively farther and farther over. The shift in the position of B and the consequent changes in GZ are shown. The accompanying graph shows the size of GZ for angles of heel through 100°, and thus provides some valuable information about this boat.

With regard to her initial stability, we see that GZ grows slowly, so the boat feels a small righting moment at low angles of heel. This means that she will heel relatively easily at first, and that she will have a gentle motion and a slow *roll period*. A boat's roll period is the time it takes for her to complete one roll to and fro, and is determined by the rate at which GZ grows. One roll will take the same amount of time whether she rolls through many degrees or only a few. Since roll period is purely a function of how GZ grows, it can serve as a handy indicator of the condition of the boat's stability, as will be seen later.

The rest of the graph shows the boat's range of stability. It indicates that GZ, and therefore the boat's tendency to right herself, increases until she reaches an angle of inclination of about 55°. As she heels beyond this point, she continues to tend to right herself but the righting moment gets weaker as GZ gets smaller. The limit of her positive stability is reached where the curve crosses the horizontal axis at 87°. At this angle of heel point B is once again vertically aligned with G and there is no GZ — no righting moment. The boat would remain in this position if nothing tipped her one way or the other. If she were pushed beyond 87°, GZ would reappear but on the opposite side of G. In that case it is said to be negative and acts to capsize the boat, not right her.

There are two other points on the curve which are of great interest. The first is the point at which the deck edge goes into the water. It is usually at this point that the curve stops being nearly linear and begins to level out. The reason for this is that up to this point as the boat heels more and more, B is moving to the right at a fairly consistent rate as more and more of the boat's volume enters the water on that side. But when the deck edge goes under and water rises on deck, the volume of boat being submerged with each degree of heel is less. This does not mean that the boat is becoming less stable, but only that her righting moment is growing at a decreasing rate.

As soon as the deck edge goes under water, it is necessary to ask at what point can water enter the boat? An undecked open boat will swamp (fill) if her deck edge goes under. A completely decked-over pontoon would have nothing to worry about, but nearly all vessels have openings in their decks to provide access, light and/or ventilation to the space below. Depending on the location and arrangement of these openings, and whether or not they are fitted with

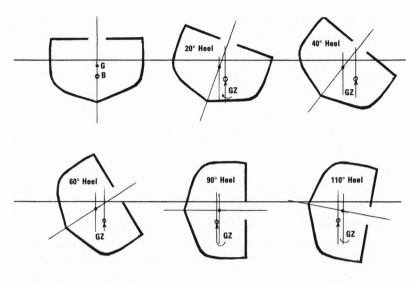

FIG. 2-7

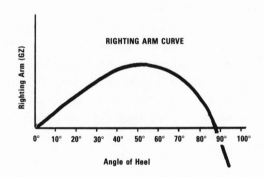

watertight closures, water may enter and sink the boat if she heels far enough.

The angle at which water would reach such an opening is called the *downflood angle,* and must be taken into account in the design and subsequent operation of any boat. In Figure 2-7 we see that although the boat has plenty of righting moment at 60°, if the centerline hatch were left open she would begin to take on water at that angle. This should suggest why openings in the deck of a boat are most often found on the centerline and not at the sides, and why they are built as high as practical above the deck.

The purpose and conditions for which the boat is intended will be the basis for deciding what will be an appropriate and safe range of stability for her. Deck edge immersion, downflood and capsize points must all be planned with safety margins in excess of the most extreme conditions she can be reasonably expected to encounter. Once the boat is built and launched, it is the responsibility of the master to ensure that she is operated within the limits her stability characteristics impose.

So far in this discussion of stability we have considered only one variable: the movement of B in response to the changing shape of hull under water. Once the boat is built, her shape is fixed and how B will move as she heels becomes a consistent and predictable phenomenon. Remember, however, that what we are talking about is a righting moment consisting of the force of buoyancy acting at the end of a lever, GZ. The length of GZ is determined not only by the position of B, but also by the position of G. If G were to move — up, down or sideways — it would alter the length of GZ in almost every situation. And G does move. In some boats G routinely moves a great deal in the course of normal operations. In others it may only move a little. In *abnormal* circumstances G can unexpectedly end up in very inappropriate places with disastrous results. We must look at how movement of G affects the boat's stability and how to keep that movement under control and within safe limits.

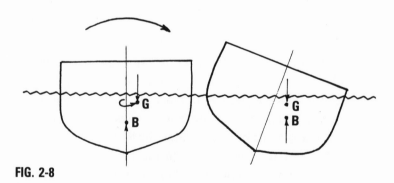

FIG. 2-8

It is not difficult to visualize how moving G will affect the boat. If it moves off to one side of center (Figure 2-8), a GZ is created which will rotate the boat to that side until B moves over the same amount.

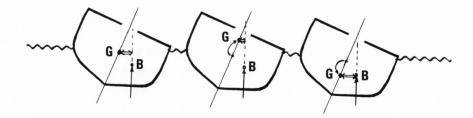

FIG. 2-9

Then the boat is in equilibrium again, but with a *list*—a constant angle of heel.

To understand the effect of raising or lowering G, look at Figure 2-9, where the boat is heeled and trying to right herself with righting arm GZ. If G were to move to a point higher in the boat, the length of GZ—the *horizontal* distance between G and B, remember—would be reduced, and she would have a smaller righting moment. We would feel this as a slower roll period. Conversely, if G were moved lower in the boat, the length of GZ would increase, giving her a greater righting moment and therefore a faster roll period.

To get a feel for how the height of G affects GZ and how this can be observed in the roll period, sit in a rocking chair. Give a push then hold your feet up. You will rock at a certain rate. Now raise your center of gravity by adding a couple of telephone books (Manhattan and Boston) to the seat. When you sit and rock again your "rock-rate" will be slower. If you went on adding books it would get slower and slower, become unstable and finally tip over.

What happened was that G got so high that GZ decreased to zero, then reappeared on the other side as a negative or capsizing arm. Notice how the slowing of the roll period is a warning of the approach of this condition. If a boat's roll period becomes abnormally slow and sluggish, it is a sure sign that GZ is smaller than normal, which in turn probably means that G is getting too high in the boat for some reason.

A boat's center of gravity is the center of all the weight of the boat, and that includes everything on or inside the boat. In all boats some part of the weight consists of things which move, or can be moved, to different positions. In the case of large cargo vessels, the moveable weight of the cargo may constitute the major part of the total weight of the loaded ship. Thus the position of G in that vessel is mostly a function of the weight and placement of her cargo.

Another example, but at the other end of the size spectrum, is a canoe. The weight of the people in it far exceeds the weight of the canoe itself, and will have an overwhelming influence on the center of gravity of the loaded vessel.

For most other types of boats, the moveable weights are a relatively small part of the total weight, but they may still have a significant effect on stability. A 25-ton yacht on a three-week voyage might carry a couple of tons of fuel, water, and supplies on board at the start of the voyage which are used up by the end. Or, at some point in her career, a new and heavy piece of equipment might be mounted on her deck. Or her main engine might be replaced by a lighter one. Any changes of this sort would bring about a change in her center of gravity. It would be necessary to reanalyze her stability in light of the change and draw a new righting arm curve in order to learn what effect the change might have on her roll period, deck edge immersion angle, downflood angle, and range of positive stability.

It is not always possible to control or even anticipate changes to the boat's center of gravity. When a half-loaded cargo vessel rolls heavily in bad weather, her cargo could break loose and shift to one side, causing the ship to list or even roll over. In a winter storm, spray may freeze on a boat's superstructure and rigging, adding more and more weight up high and thus raising G. An alert master would notice his boat's roll period getting slower and make every effort to get rid of the ice before stability was lost.

Fuel and water tanks which are partially full will cause a change in the position of G as the liquid sloshes from side to side in the tank with the motion of the boat. This is known as the *free surface effect*. To control and minimize this effect, baffles are built into tanks to dampen the sloshing action. In addition, it is good practice to draw fuel and water from just one tank at a time, keeping the rest either completely full or completely empty.

Finally, any damage the boat sustains which alters the distribution of her weight will have implications for her stability. If she takes on water from a collision or grounding—or perhaps from water being intentionally pumped into her while fighting a fire—G will be affected both by the weight of the water and by the free surface effect that will occur in the bilges. It is likely that long before a boat took on enough water to sink, she would lose her positive righting arm and capsize.

SUMMARY

Stability is a boat's tendency to return to an upright position when she is heeled by an external force. Initial stability refers to the quality of that tendency as the boat is heeled through small angles. The terms stiff and tender are matched with a quick roll period and a slow roll period respectively, and describe a boat's initial stability. Range of stability refers to her response to large angles of heel, and includes the critical points of deck edge immersion, downflood and capsize.

The tendency, known as a righting moment, is caused by the interaction of the weight of the boat (force of gravity) and the opposing upthrust of the water (force of buoyancy). These two forces are considered to act at their respective centers (G and B), and when there is horizontal separation between them, a righting arm (GZ) exists. The force of buoyancy acting upward at the end of this lever works to rotate the boat.

Since the force of buoyancy is essentially constant, the strength of the righting moment at any given time is primarily determined by the length of GZ. This length in turn is determined by the positions of G and B. How B will move is the naval architect's responsibility since that is a function of the underwater shape of the boat. The position of G, however, is the master's concern as he loads, unloads, handles, and sails his boat. Much about stability can be calculated and predicted, but much also has to be sensed and decided on the basis of the boat's behavior at sea in various conditions. In this regard her roll period is the most valuable on-the-spot indicator of her stability.

As with everything, experience is an important ingredient in developing a sixth sense about stability. After the rocking chair, try a canoe—in warm shallow water—and experiment with GZ!

CHAPTER THREE

The Theory of Sail

The sailboat is an energy converter. She floats on the interface between two fluids, water and air, and by interacting with each is able to extract energy from their movement. We have learned how to build and handle the boat so that this energy will propel her anywhere we want to go on the sea.

We tend to think of the propelling force as coming from the wind, with the water as a resistance to be overcome. Practically, this view is fine and will enable us to sail our boat well. For understanding just how the sailboat works, however, it is a somewhat misleading viewpoint. It is only half the picture, because it would be equally accurate to say that the water flowing past the hull propels the boat through the air! The reality is a combination of both: energy is available because of the *relative movement* of the air and water. The sailing boat can capture and utilize that energy by offering resistance to *both* fluids, by means of her sail in the air and her hull in the water.

Moreover, the sailboat uses the same process both in the air and in the water to produce the forces that propel her. In turn, we will look at what is happening in the air with the sails and in the water with the hull, then see how the two phenomena combine to enable the boat to go. Since we will be talking about the same forces both above and below the sea surface, we will need to distinguish between them, and therefore will adopt the point of view that sees the wind as the source of the *propelling* force and the water a source of

41

resisting forces. Forces generated by the sails will be labelled F, and those generated by the hull, R.

IN THE AIR

We can begin very simply, as early man must have begun his sailing, by getting on a log and letting the wind blow us along. There is nothing tricky here: the wind blowing against us results in a force, F (Figure 3-1).

FIG. 3-1

According to the basic rules, when an object is acted on by a force it accelerates in the direction of that force. So we pick up speed in the direction the wind is blowing. But as soon as the log begins to move it feels resistance from the water. The resistance increases as the log moves faster until it matches the propelling force of the wind. Then the log accelerates no more, and we sail *downwind* at a steady speed (Figure 3-2)

That was easy because we expect the wind to produce a force in the direction it is blowing, and we expect an object to go in the

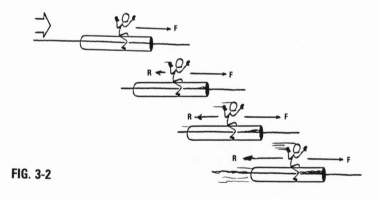

FIG. 3-2

direction it is pulled or pushed. Easy, but rather limited: if all we could do with a sailboat was go downwind, we would not consider sailing to be a viable means of getting across the harbor, let alone hundreds or thousands of miles across oceans. But sailing vessels are not limited to sailing *with* the wind. If you have not already experienced it, you will soon realize that modern sailboats can go in many directions other than downwind. The other directions possible are shown in Figure 3-3 and given names. From this it can be seen that a sailboat can actually be propelled by the wind in directions not only *across* the wind, but even somewhat *into* the wind.

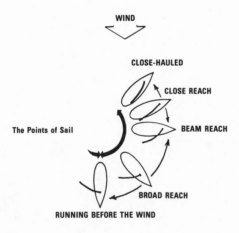

FIG. 3-3

How can that be? If the wind provides the propelling force, how can it bring about motion apparently against itself? All *points of sail* other than *running before the wind* require an answer to that question in order to be understood. We will concentrate on an explanation of the most extreme case—that of the *close reach*—and the other points of sail will become clear along the way.

The answer we will find is in two parts. In the first place, objects in a fluid flow may not always feel a simple downstream force. Wind blowing past a sail, for example, can result in a force in some other direction. Secondly, it is only our point of view that causes us to see the wind as the sole source of a propelling force. Although we will be calling it "resistance," the forces produced by the water flowing past the hull of the boat contribute as well to the direction in which the boat is propelled.

Blow a Ping-Pong ball across the table (Figure 3-4). It goes in the direction you blow.

FIG. 3-4

Hold your hand out the window of the car and tilt it about 45° to the wind. It is both dragged back and lifted up. The overall effect is a tendency for it to move in a direction as shown in Figure 3-5.

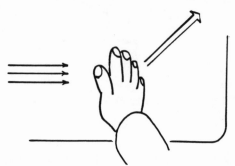

FIG. 3-5

Here then are two objects responding quite differently to a fluid flowing past them. What accounts for the different directions they are pushed relative to the flow direction?

The difference is the shape around which the air must travel. If we could see the flow around the ball and the hand, they would look something like Figure 3-6.

The flow pattern past the round ball is symmetrical, while past the flat and tilted hand the pattern is asymmetrical. On the upper side of the hand the air is pushed farther out of its way, and thus it

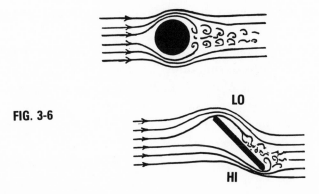

FIG. 3-6

has farther to go than the air below. Since both the air above and the air below pass the hand in the same amount of time, the upper air must move faster in order to cover a greater distance.

Daniel Bernoulli in the 18th century discovered that a moving fluid exerts less *sideways* pressure than one at rest, and that the faster a fluid flows, the less pressure it exerts. This is observable in many common phenomena, but the easiest demonstration of the effect is to hold a sheet of paper to your chin, just below your lower lip, and blow over the top of it. The paper will rise. It rises because, when you blow, the pressure in the moving stream of air drops to less than the pressure of the still air under the paper. This pressure difference is felt by the paper as a force which pushes it upward.

The flow of air around your hand out the car window is such that the air above your hand is moving faster than that below it. This reduces the pressure above relative to that below, and an upward force is felt. The upward force is only part of what you feel, however. The other part is the simple downstream force of the wind dragging your hand back. The two together cause your hand to move in the direction that it does. In other words, the *total force* felt by your hand consists of two components: one is acting at right angles to the direction of the flow (upwards, in this case) and is called *lift*. The other is acting parallel to the flow (downstream) and is called *drag*. Pure drag is what moved the Ping-Pong ball downwind, and is always present. Lift will result when an asymmetrical flow pattern causes a pressure differential. On the side where the flow is accelerated, the pressure will be reduced, and a lift force will be felt by the object in the direction of the low pressure at right angles to the flow.

Representing these forces by vectors helps us visualize how they behave under various conditions. The *total force* (F_t) in Figure 3-7 represents what the object actually feels as the result of the flow around it. F_t will always consist of lift and drag in various proportions, and will be drawn as the diagonal of a rectangle whose sides are lift and drag. Remember that the direction of the lift and drag forces is determined by the direction of the fluid flow — wind, in this case — because by definition they are forces perpendicular and parallel to the flow respectively.

FIG. 3-7

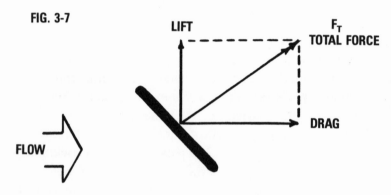

Of what significance is this to sailing? Simply this: if we have been looking for a force to propel our boat in directions other than just downwind, we have found one. Place a sail in the wind, adjust it so that it presents an asymmetrical aspect to the flow, and in addition to the inescapable component of drag pulling downwind, we now find a component of lift pulling across the wind, so that their sum — the total force produced by the sail — pulls in a direction at an angle to the wind's direction.

In Figure 3-8 the view is from above looking at a cross section of a sail. With reference to the wind, lift is at right angles and drag is in line. F_t is the direction the sail will try to move. It is a force which could be used to move the boat.

The obvious next question is what is the range of directions relative to the wind that we can sail using an F_t from a sail? We should be able to move in any direction that we can get F_t to point,

FIG. 3-8

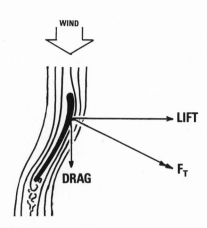

so what we are really asking is what is the range of F_t's we can produce with a sail in a given wind?

Since F_t is the sum of a lift force and a drag force, it can theoretically range from all drag and no lift, to all lift and no drag, including all the combinations in between.

In fact, it is possible to arrange a sail to produce all drag and no lift. As long as it presents a symmetrical aspect to the wind, no lift will occur. The total force resulting will be straight downwind.

On the other hand, it is *not* possible to eliminate drag completely from any real situation. There will always be some downwind component resulting from friction, turbulence and all the inefficiencies that separate reality from the ideal! Therefore, although we can *approach* all lift and no drag, F_t can never pull directly across the wind. The range of theoretically possible F_t's is from straight downwind to as close to across the wind as we can manage. We must now look closely at sails and find out just what determines the ratio of lift to drag that they produce. Since we want to extend the range of directions as much as possible, we are especially interested in how to get a high ratio of lift to drag, to make F_t as close as possible to a crosswind force.

Since lift on a sail is the result of a faster airflow on one side than the other, anything that increases that difference will increase lift. We have already recognized that the shape of the object in the flow is important. If it is symmetrical, the flow will be, too, and no lift will occur. Therefore, it must be asymmetrical. But of all asymmetrical shapes, some are clearly better than others. Your hand, a basically flat surface tilted to the wind, was adequate to produce *some* lift. But a closer look at the flow pattern around a flat surface shows that air does not have an easy time moving suddenly around sharp corners. Air molecules, like anything else, have inertia and resist changes in speed and direction. When forced to make abrupt changes, an airflow will cease flowing in a smooth stream and become disorganized or turbulent. When this happens the flow loses velocity. Thus in Figure 3-6 at the point where the flow became turbulent, it stopped being faster than the flow beneath the surface, and from that point back no lift was produced. A flat surface is not the best shape for generating a lot of lift.

We will also notice that if we tilt our hand at different angles to the wind we feel changes in the lift force on it. At some angles the airstream over the top is accelerated more than at others, and at some angles the stream, unable to travel around a sharp corner, separates and becomes turbulent.

It seems that two things are key to keeping the flow smooth and attached to the surface. One is the *shape* of the surface, and the other is the *angle of attack* between the flow and the surface. With the help of a graph we can study the effect of changes in each of these variables on the ratio of lift to drag produced by a sail.

In Figure 3-9 the vertical axis represents lift and the horizontal axis, drag. A line from zero to any point on the graph is a vector representing the F_t produced by the surface we are studying, which is in an airstream at the angle of attack shown.

We now rotate the surface through 90°—from straight into the wind to flat across it—and plot the ratio of lift to drag produced at each 15° angle of attack. The F_t for each of these positions is readily found by connecting each point to zero, and connecting all the points together results in a curve which describes the Lift/Drag ratio for this particular surface at all angles of attack (Figure 3-10).

Let us first look at how changing angle of attack affects the L/D ratio, and thereby F_t. At 0° angle of attack, the surface is aligned with the wind, presenting the least resistance and a symmetrical aspect. The graph shows a small F_t comprised of some drag and no

FIG. 3-9

FIG. 3-10

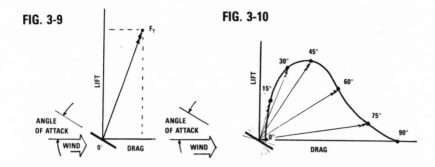

lift. At 90° the aspect is again symmetrical so there is no lift, but this time drag is at a maximum. For every angle in between 0° and 90° there is asymmetrical flow and a combination of lift and drag results. The ratio of lift to drag in each case is a function of how much the flow is accelerated over the top of the surface. As the angle increases from 0° the airflow is accelerated more and more until it can no longer stay attached and lift is lost. As the graph shows this occurs at about the 45° angle of attack.

From a sailing point of view this graph tells us that if this particular surface were a sail, it would produce its highest ratio of lift to drag at about a 30° angle of attack. In order to propel our boat as nearly across the wind as possible, this is the angle at which we should trim our sail to the wind.

The correct angle of attack is important for maximizing lift, but equally important is the shape of the surface. As suggested already, a fluid stream has a difficult time with sharp corners. Therefore, if the surface it is to follow is curved gradually, and changes shape smoothly, the flow will follow it better. The surface should curve just enough to keep coaxing the flow into going faster, yet not so much that the flow gives up trying and becomes turbulent. The classic "airfoil" shape which is found in birds' wings, airplane wings, propellers and the like is the ideal shape to do this. A well-made sail seen in cross section is this shape.

The airfoil shape can actually take many forms and it is the sailmaker's business to design and build the best shaped sail *for the purpose for which it is intended.* In other words, there is no one best shape. The graph in Figure 3-11 compares the L/D ratios of two different shapes.

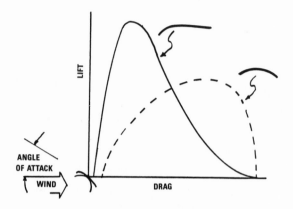

FIG. 3-11

Figure 3-12 shows how the lift force is distributed over a typical sail. Because the flow is faster in some regions than in others, there is a bigger pressure differential and thus more lift in those areas. As we can see, the foil-shaped sail produces most of its lift in the forward third of its area — near the leading edge — where the curvature is greatest. The rest of the sail is relatively insignificant as far as the production of lift is concerned. The value of the rest of the sail comes in when we want to maximize the drag component for sailing downwind. In that case, what is wanted is just plain *area* to produce lots of drag. An example of how differently shaped sails serve different purposes is to look at the overall evolution of sail shape through the ages from the first square sail to today's high-tech racing sails.

The earliest sails were probably relatively shapeless pieces of surface area hung up to produce drag. At first this was because nothing better was known and vessels were limited to sailing downwind, relying on oars and muscle to go other directions. Later, these square sails persisted and were preferred for the ships that logged most of their miles sailing downwind in the world's reliable wind routes. But for the vessels doing more local and coastwise voyages in

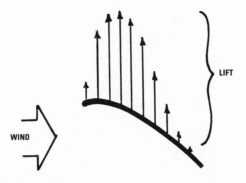

FIG. 3-12

regions where the wind might blow from any direction, sails evolved which could move them effectively in more and more directions away from just downwind. These sails had to produce lift, and as it became apparent that lift happened along the leading edges of foil-shaped sails, there was an evolution from square, to gaff-headed, to marconi-type sails (Figure 3-13), and, as mast-building and supporting technology advanced, they got steadily taller and taller—to get more of that leading edge. The term *aspect ratio* describes the ratio of a sail's height to its width, and it is generally true that the higher the aspect ratio of a sail, the higher its L/D ratio will be.

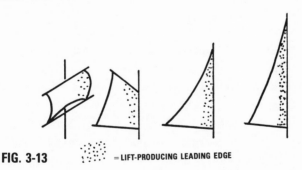

FIG. 3-13 = LIFT-PRODUCING LEADING EDGE

There is one more means of improving a sail's L/D ratio that we need to know about. That is the use of one sail to direct the flow of wind onto another, and is known as the *slot effect*. The sail in Figure

3-14 is not effective at the angle of attack shown, but when the other sail is set ahead of it, the air stream is concentrated and remains attached, thus greatly improving the sail's performance. On a vessel with many sails it is very important that each one be trimmed correctly to maximize its effect on the ones behind it.

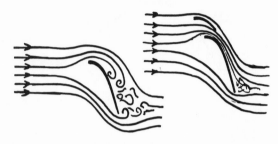

FIG. 3-14

Our understanding of the forces produced by a surface in a fluid flow enables us to choose a sail with an appropriate shape, and set it at an optimum angle of attack to the wind to produce a total force (F_t) that can range from straight downwind to close to—but never quite—across the wind. If we were to mount the sail on an object that was free to move in response to any force applied to it, we could use that F_t to propel the object in that same range of directions. A round salad bowl floating in the water might be such an object . . .

IN THE WATER

Push the salad bowl in some direction and it will accelerate in that direction. Imagine a sail on the salad bowl making an F_t as shown in Figure 3-15 and you would see the salad bowl begin to move in the direction of F_t.

Now, if you have sailed—and quite possibly even if you have not—you probably are aware that a) sailboats can sail in directions closer to the direction from which the wind is blowing than 90°, and b) sailboats are not shaped like salad bowls. Not surprisingly, there is a cause and effect relationship here which, to understand properly, requires that we look at what goes on in the other fluid—the water—as the sailboat responds to the F_t from her sail.

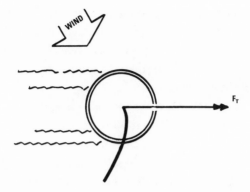

FIG. 3-15

When something moves through the water, water flows past it. It is simply a question of point of view again. Here (Figure 3-16) is the salad bowl responding to a force, F_t. It accelerates, and after a certain amount of time the situation would look as shown.

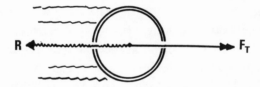

FIG. 3-16

The bowl is moving; water is flowing past it, and this flow has produced a downstream resistance force, R, equal and opposite to F_t, so we know that the bowl is moving at a steady speed and direction. In the air with the sail, we called a downstream force drag, and this resistance from the water, which is in line with the water flow, we call drag also. Just as it was impossible to escape drag in the air, there is no way to avoid it in the water either, but there are some ways to reduce it and thereby enable a boat to move more easily through the water.

There are principally two kinds of drag resistance a hull will feel as it moves through the water. The first of these is simple *friction*, seen as a layer of turbulent water next to the moving hull. If the hull is rough-surfaced, has sharp corners or abrupt changes of curvature which the flow cannot follow, or is covered with weeds and barnacles, this friction will be unnecessarily great. Designing a hull with smooth "fair" curves, and then keeping the bottom clean will reduce this kind of drag.

The other kind of drag resistance a hull will encounter is called *wave-making* resistance. When a boat moves through the water it must push the water aside and then bring it back together again, so some of the energy meant for propelling the boat is used up moving large masses of water to and fro. This energy, when transferred to the water this way, shows as a system of waves which emanate from the boat. This is called the boat's *wake*. In general, the faster the boat goes, the larger will be the wake that she makes. Up to a point, the resistance the boat feels from making these waves is roughly proportional to her speed.

Sooner or later, however, as the boat goes faster another factor enters the picture. This is the phenomenon called *hull speed*. The length (from crest to crest) of the transverse wave that is formed along the boat's side is strictly a function of her speed through the water, and the wave gets longer as the boat goes faster. Figure 3-17 shows what happens as the boat gains speed. At some speed the wavelength will begin to be longer than the boat's waterline length. When this happens the stern of the boat will drop down into the trough of the wave. Now if the boat is to go any faster, she must literally climb the hill of her own bow wave. For all but very high-powered craft designed to plane (skim) on the surface of the water, this is practically if not theoretically impossible.

The speed at which the wave produced by the boat matches her waterline length is called her hull speed. This speed is a function of her waterline length, and can be found for any vessel by the formula:

Hull Speed (in knots) = 1.34 × Waterline Length (in feet)

The graph in Figure 3-18 compares the relative significance of frictional and wave-making resistance over a range of speeds for a boat about 50 feet on the waterline. Frictional resistance can be

seen to vary fairly directly with speed, while wave-making resistance suddenly becomes an all but insurmountable obstacle to
further acceleration at about 9½ knots.

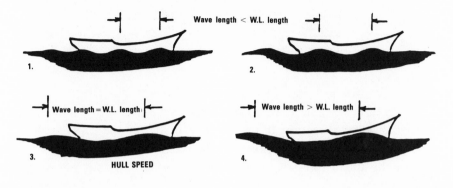

FIG. 3-17

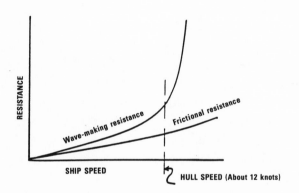

FIG. 3-18

These two kinds of resistance are drag forces by definition: they
act parallel to the flow of the water. In the case of a power driven
vessel, a boat being towed, or a sailboat with the wind blowing
from directly behind her, they are the only sources of resistance that
will appear. In all those instances, the propelling F_t is pulling
straight ahead along the boat's centerline, and as she moves forward
the flow past her hull is the same on both sides—symmetrical.

Now suppose the F_t was not pulling straight ahead but off
somewhat to one side. The salad bowl in this case would still move

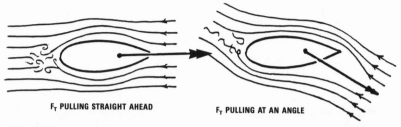

F$_T$ PULLING STRAIGHT AHEAD   F$_T$ PULLING AT AN ANGLE

FIG. 3-19

in the direction of F$_t$, but a salad bowl is a symmetrical shape no matter what direction it moves. The boat, on the other hand, presents a symmetrical aspect to the water *only* when she moves straight ahead (or straight astern). When she responds to the F$_t$ shown in the second picture of Figure 3-19 by moving in that direction, the water flowing past her strikes her at an angle that makes her an asymmetrical shape. Thus the flow that develops around her is also asymmetrical. In fact, the pattern of that flow should look very familiar by now. We are seeing an object whose shape and angle of attack cause the fluid which is moving past it to be accelerated on one side! Bernoulli's principle is as valid in the water as it was in the air, so where the water on one side moves faster it causes low pressure there relative to the other side. This, of course, means that the hull feels a force on it acting towards the low pressure, pushing it sideways at right angles to the flow of water. This is *hydrodynamic lift*.

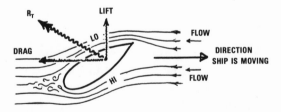

FIG. 3-20

Just as with the sail in the air, we now find that the hull in the water is producing lift and drag forces of its own. They are components of what we call the *total resistance* (R$_t$) which the hull feels, and are shown by vectors as well. In Figure 3-20 the hull is moving in the direction shown. The asymmetrical water flow around it produces some lift and some drag which, taken together, comprise the total resistance, R_t. Like the F_t from our sail, this R_t can range in direction from straight downstream (pure drag) to something approaching right angles to the stream (again, pure lift is impossible). All the factors we have discussed in connection with hull resistance will determine the ratio of lift to drag for a hull in a given situation. An important point to remember is that when the hull moves straight ahead, flow is symmetrical and R_t is all drag. Only when the hull moves at an angle does it present an asymmetrical aspect and produce any lift.

TOGETHER ON THE INTERFACE

Before we put it all together, let us review our ultimate objective and take stock of what we have to work with.

What are we trying to do? We are trying to extend the range of directions the sailboat can sail as much as we can, thus making her more versatile and useful. First we saw that sailing downwind is simple. Then, when we found that we could vary the direction of F_t, a variety of courses from downwind to slightly less than across the wind became available. Is it possible to do still better—sail closer to the wind's direction? It is, and so the question is: How?

We have two forces which can be made to work on our boat. Although we have named one F_t and think of it as a propelling force, and the other R_t, and think of it as a resisting force, the boat knows no difference between them. Bound to the laws of physics, the boat's response to *any* force that acts on it is the same: accelerate in that direction as a good body must!

We have some degree of control over F_t and R_t. Within certain limits we can point them over a range of directions depending on how we design, build and rig our boat, and how we set and trim the sails and steer the hull through the water.

Two forces, some control over them, and a body which must respond to them according to the rules. . . .

To understand how a boat can sail closer to the wind than the F_t

from her sails we will put together a frame-by-frame sequence of glimpses of the boat starting from a standstill and ending up sailing steadily on a *close-hauled* course (about 50° off the wind's direction). The forces acting on the boat will be made visible as vectors pulling this way and that.

Here is the boat (Figure 3-21), her sail set, waiting for the wind. Because we are trying to sail as close to the wind as possible, we have set and trimmed the sail to give us the highest possible L/D ratio from the north wind that is forecast. That will ensure that F_t will be as close as we can make it to east, and also as close as possible to our heading, northeast.

FIG. 3-21

The wind comes from the north, and Frame 1 of Figure 3-22 shows how the sail produces F_t. This will not change during the rest of this sequence, so for clarity we will omit all but the F_t vector from the rest of the frames. If you forget where it comes from or why it points in the direction it does, refer back to this frame. Otherwise, consider F_t a steady force, pulling like a towrope to accelerate the boat.

In Frame 2 we see the boat's response to F_t: she starts to move in the direction she is pulled: east-southeast. This means that a flow of water begins past the hull *from the direction toward which the boat is moving*. As a result of this flow the hull begins to feel drag (downstream), and because the flow is asymmetrical, lift (across the stream). The sum of these two, R_t, is shown.

So when we arrive at Frame 2 the boat is being acted on by two "total" forces, F_t and R_t, pulling in the directions and amounts shown by their vectors. When a body is affected by two forces simultaneously, we can show the net result as a single vector which is the diagonal of the parallelogram formed by using the two

FIG. 3-22

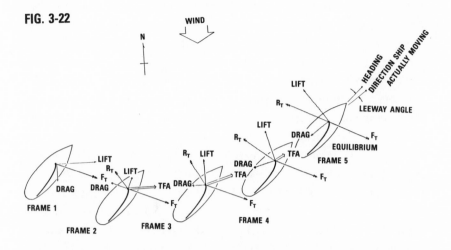

components as sides. Adding the two forces F_t and R_t in frame 2 gives us a vector which we can call the *total force of acceleration* (TFA). This is net direction and amount that the boat is accelerating at this moment.

Notice that even within this frame a change has occurred. At first the boat was moved only by F_t (TFA = F_t) because *until she began to move* there was no R_t. So her first movement was toward F_t, or east-southeast. As soon as there was an R_t, however, its effect had to be added to that of F_t and the TFA began to change.

As we enter Frame 3 we find the boat moving through the water toward the east in response to the TFA from Frame 2. The flow, therefore, is from that direction, which means a different angle of attack for the hull, different flow pattern, and different L/D ratio. In addition, the boat is gaining speed, so the forces produced by the hull in the water are all larger. (Notice that the lift and drag vectors must always be oriented with respect to the flow direction.) Their sum, R_t, is now larger, and when added to the unchanged F_t, gives a TFA which is smaller in size, but again pulling more forward. In response to this TFA, she will continue to accelerate, though less than before, and she will move in the direction of east-northeast.

In Frame 4 she is now moving east-northeast as can be seen by the change of flow direction (and consequently, angle of attack and L/D ratio). She is also moving faster as shown by the larger sizes of the lift, drag and R_t vectors. Now R_t is nearly as big as F_t, and when they are added they yield a TFA that is very small. What is happening?

The boat is approaching equilibrium. There is a TFA so she *will* accelerate a bit more, and since it is pointed still more forward, she will change her direction of travel to almost northeast, but then in Frame 5 it happens . . .

With the boat moving *almost* in the direction she is pointed, we add F_t and R_t and get zero—no TFA. They are equal and opposite; the boat has reached a state of equilibrium where all the forces from the wind and water are in balance. In order to achieve this state she has had to reach this particular speed (whatever it is—we cannot tell from these drawings) and be moving in this particular direction. Now, in equilibrium, she will continue on this course and speed until something changes and the forces become unbalanced.

The wind might change strength or direction; someone might trim the sail differently: F_t would be affected. The helmsman might steer her to a new course; she might reach hull speed, or barnacles might grow on her bottom: R_t would change. Any change in any of the forces involved would cause the boat's course and speed to change, which would in turn alter the rest of the forces until equilibrium was restored. In practice, all the forces are constantly changing, and equilibrium is never sustained for long. Only by continually adjusting F_t and R_t can the boat be kept steady on her course.

As just one example of this, here is a sequence showing how a wind shift might affect the boat's progress (Figure 3-23). Frame 1 shows the boat sailing in equilibrium as close to the wind as she can. She is heading northeast (045°) but actually moving 050°, so her angle of attack with the water is 5°. This is also called her *leeway*.

The wind shifts from north to northwest. Frame 2 shows the effect of the new wind direction if no action was taken by the crew in response. While the sail's angle of attack was ideal for a high L/D ratio in the north wind, it is now much too great in the northwest wind. The airflow has become turbulent, lift has been lost, and the result is mostly drag as seen by the change in direction of F_t. This

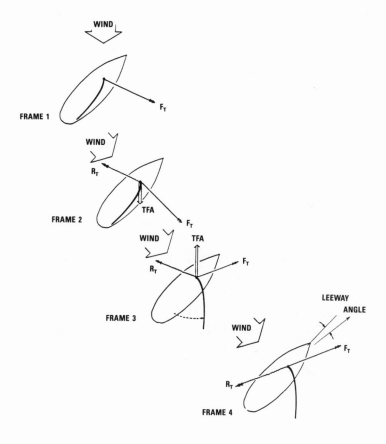

FIG. 3-23

new F_t, together with the old R_t add up to a TFA that acts to slow the boat down and pull her sideways. If left alone she would end up in an equilibrium where she was slowly sliding sideways downwind. We would say that the sail was *over trimmed* for the wind; it is hauled in too flat. The result is loss of forward speed and excessive leeway.

The appropriate response to a wind shift like this is to adjust the sail so as to maintain the best angle of attack. This can be done either by turning the whole boat and going in a new direction, or if we wish to continue in the same direction, by trimming the sail. In Frame 3 we have trimmed the sail so that its angle of attack is optimal for the new wind. Now F_t points much farther ahead than it did with the old wind. Together with the R_t at this moment it makes a TFA acting to the north. Of course the instant the boat begins to accelerate in this direction, the flow around the hull becomes more symmetrical and hydrodynamic lift drops off. R_t swings back reflecting the greater ratio of drag to lift, and a new equilibrium is reached (Frame 4) with the boat moving faster and with less leeway than before the wind shifted.

It is important to realize that except in cases where F_t can be made to point *straight ahead,* a sailboat will have to make some leeway. If the boat did not go slightly sideways, the flow past her hull would not be asymmetrical. Then there would be no sideways lift force in the water to counter the sideways pull of F_t, and . . . the boat would go sideways! So, if she did not go sideways a little, she would go sideways a lot. Good sails, hull design, proper sail trim, and good helmsmanship all help to keep this inevitable leeway angle small—normally only a few degrees—but it must be there.

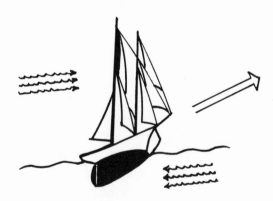

CHAPTER FOUR

Shiphandling Under Sail

The purpose of this chapter is to take everything we have seen in the way of forces at work on a sailboat, and describe in seagoing terms how they are managed on board. Controlling these forces is the activity we call *sailing,* the ultimate object of which is to make the boat do what we want her to do — go this way or that, go faster or slower, stop, turn around, or whatever. The forces involved are F_t and R_t, and controlling them means handling the sails and steering the hull. We will therefore look at what means we as sailors on the boat have to do this.

STEERING

The boat is steered by the *rudder,* a hinged flap at the stern which is moved either directly by a *tiller,* or through a system of ropes or gears by a *wheel.* It diverts the flow of water coming by the hull and imparts a sideways force resulting from the asymmetrical flow around it (heard of it?) to the stern of the boat. This causes the boat to pivot and change her heading (Figure 4-1).

Two important points about the rudder are that its effectiveness is dependent upon a flow of water past it, and that the boat is turned (that is, her bow swings) to the same side the rudder is moved. The rudder becomes less and less effective as the boat slows down, and if she is not moving at all through the water, the rudder is utterly powerless to turn the boat. If you forget that, there will come a time when you will have the rudder hard over and wonder why there is no

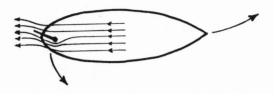

RUDDER

FIG. 4-1

response from the boat . . . until you glance over the side and realize that no water is flowing past.

There are other ways to turn the boat, as we will see. They can overwhelm the rudder's effect, so it must only be considered an *aid* to steering and not the positive control that a car's steering wheel offers.

SAIL HANDLING

The term sail handling refers to 1) *setting* and *striking* sails (pulling them up and pulling them down) and 2) *trimming* sails (adjusting their angle of attack to the wind, and thereby the direction in which their forces act).

A sail is set by hauling on its *halyard* (Figure 4-2). This is a line attached to the head of a sail, leading over a block somewhere aloft, and back down to the deck. The sail is struck by releasing the halyard and either hauling the sail down, or in the case of a large sail, hauling a *downhaul,* another line attached to the sail's head but leading directly down to the deck.

FIG. 4-2

When a sail is set in the wind, it will want to blow in line with the wind and flap like a flag. This is called *luffing.* A sail which is luffing is not producing any useful force. To make the sail *fill* (stop luffing) and go to work, its free corner, the *clew* must be controlled. This is done by a line called a *sheet.* Hauling the sheet stretches the sail, causing it to fill at some angle of attack to the wind. This angle, and to some extent the shape of the sail, can be adjusted by hauling in or slacking out the sheet. This is trimming the sail.

Depending on the boat's heading relative to the wind direction, the sails are sheeted to one side or the other of the boat. If the wind is coming from some direction over her port side, she is said to be on the *port tack.* In that case her sails will be sheeted to starboard. If she is on the *starboard tack,* they will be sheeted to port (Figure 4-3).

To accommodate both possibilities, most sails have two sheets attached to their clews, one leading to each side of the boat, but only one in use at time. If the sail's foot is attached to a *boom,* however, a single sheet is sufficient for both tacks.

Halyards, downhauls, and sheets comprise most of a boat's *run-*

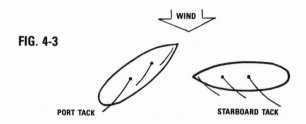

FIG. 4-3

ning rigging—the lines that are handled in sailing the boat. On a large vessel where the sails are heavy and their forces are large, most of the halyards and sheets are rigged with a substantial mechanical advantage through blocks and tackles and/or winches to enable us to manage them. Figure 4-4 shows some typical arrangements for a halyard and a sheet.

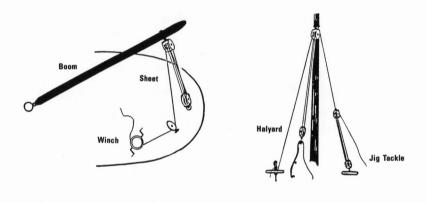

FIG. 4-4

WHICH SAILS TO SET

To make the boat go, sails must be set. But which ones? On a large vessel such as the stays'l schooner in Figure 4-5 there are five to choose among. On smaller boats there will be fewer, but the principles governing which to choose are the same. Two considerations enter into that choice, and we will look into them both:

1) How strong is the wind and/or how fast do we want to go?

2) What direction is the wind blowing relative to the direction we wish to go, that is, what point of sail will we be on?

A sailboat must be designed with enough sail area so that she can move in very light winds. As the wind increases she will go faster, but at some wind speed, unless she reduces that area by taking in some sails, she will reach the limits of efficiency and safety. For example, she may approach hull speed, and no matter how hard her sails pull, not be able to go any faster. She will heel farther as the wind increases and may reach critical points on her stability curve—deck edge immersion, downflood, etc. Or sails, rigging, and spars may simply break from too much stress. The decision of how much sail to carry requires familiarity with the boat's characteristics.

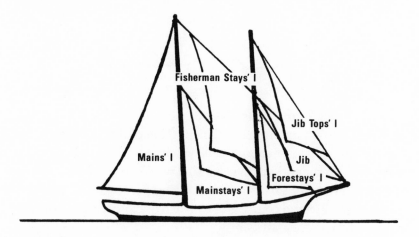

FIG. 4-5

Sails are usually struck in order of highest to lowest. This is because the force of the wind increases significantly from the sea surface upward, so that if it is blowing 20 knots on deck, it is probably blowing 25 knots at the masthead 50 feet above the deck. The upper sails are there to take advantage of this fact when the wind is light. They are built of lighter material and their sheets and halyards are lighter as well. Being highest, they have the greatest leverage on the hull, so when they pull sideways they have a big heeling effect on the boat. Our stays'l schooner would strike her *fisherman stays'l* and *jib tops'l* first in response to a rising wind.

Another means of reducing sail area is by *reefing* a sail. If the sail is made to be reefed, it can be made smaller by mechanically rolling it up around its boom or stay, or by *tying in a reef* by hand. The mains'l shown in Figure 4-6 has two rows of holes sewn into it so that it can be reefed down to two different sizes. The sail is lowered, and a new foot is made by tying down one of the rows to the boom. The remainder of the sail is then reset.

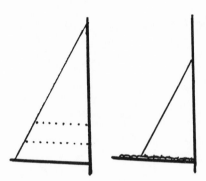

FIG. 4-6

After taking into account the strength of the wind, we choose which sails to set according to the direction of the wind relative to our heading. We must choose sails which together will balance the boat for that point of sail. In general, if we are to sail downwind we will concentrate the sail area in the forward part of the rig, and if we are to sail an upwind course—close reach or close hauled—then we will want more area aft.

To understand this, picture the boat stopped in the water, broadside to the wind with no sails set. If we then hoist the *mainsail* and trim the sheet, how would the boat respond? Because the mains'l is so far aft, the force it produces will have a strong *turning* effect on the boat. Her stern will be pushed downwind, and she will pivot like a weathervane, swinging her bow into the wind.

If instead of the mains'l we set the *headsails,* the opposite will happen: the boat's bow will be pulled around, away from the wind. In each case the sail exerts a turning force pivoting the boat around an imaginary point called her *center of lateral resistance* (CLR).

The CLR is the geometric center of the underwater part of the hull as seen in profile (see Figure 4-7). Forces from sails located aft of the CLR will tend to rotate her *into* the wind; forces from sails forward of the CLR will tend to turn her *away* from it.

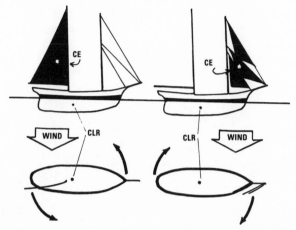

FIG. 4-7

Each sail also has a geometric center, which is where the force produced by the sail is considered to act. This is called the *center of effort* (CE) of the sail. When more than one sail is set, their individual CE's can be combined to locate an overall CE for the boat (Figure 4-7). Thus for any group of sails we choose to set we can calculate—or estimate—their combined CE, and if we then see where that lies in relation to the boat's CLR, we can tell what if any turning effect the boat will feel. If the CE is close to the CLR the turning effect will be small; the farther they are separated horizontally the greater it will be.

A sail plan is said to be balanced for a given point of sail when its overall CE is in a position relative to the CLR that makes the boat *"want"* to go in the desired direction without a lot of force from the rudder. If it is not reasonably well balanced, the boat will be difficult, perhaps impossible, to steer. The turning effect of the sails can easily overpower the rudder, and in any case it is inefficient to have to use a big rudder angle to keep the boat on her heading. If she is hard to steer, the chances are the sail balance can be made better by a different choice of sails.

Figure 4-8 shows sail plans for our schooner that are balanced for reaching, close-reaching, and sailing close-hauled in various strengths of wind. The CE is close to the CLR so that the boat steers easily. When she heels she will tend to turn into the wind but only a small amount of rudder angle is needed to compensate for this.

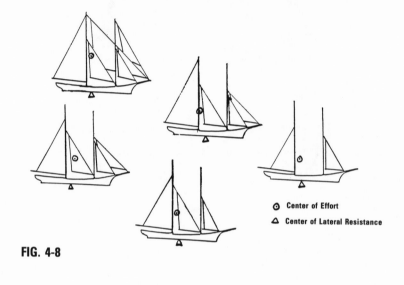

⊙ Center of Effort

△ Center of Lateral Resistance

FIG. 4-8

FIG. 4-9

Figure 4-9 shows sail plans that are balanced for sailing off the wind—broad-reaching and running. The CE is well forward so that the boat's bow will be pulled downwind. The rudder will be needed only to keep her on a precise course.

It is impossible to sail close to the wind with the CE very far forward of the CLR—nothing but a lot of leeway would result. Conversely, sailing downwind with the CE aft makes for very difficult steering and the danger that the sails may overpower the rudder and swing the boat around into the wind out of control.

TRIMMING SAILS

Once having determined which sails to set, the next question is how should they be trimmed—that is, how tightly should their clews be hauled in by their sheets?

Again it is a question of wind direction relative to desired boat's heading. The objective is to propel the boat as efficiently as possible, so we want to make the F_t from each sail point as far forward as we can. As shown in Figure 4-10, there is a range of trim possibilities for each sail from as far in as it can be stretched to as far out as it go without either luffing or hitting some other part of the boat ahead of it. For the mains'l, this is usually the point at which the boom hits the *shrouds* (wire rigging supporting the mast), and normally means that the mains'l cannot be let out more than about 60°. Somewhere between these extremes is the correct trim for the sail.

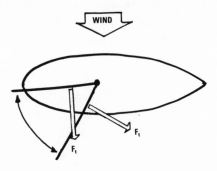

FIG. 4-10

The way to find the proper set for any point of sail *other than close-hauled* is this:

With the boat on the desired heading, slowly ease out the sheet. You will be changing the sail's angle of attack to the wind, improving its lift/drag ratio, and thereby pointing F_t more and more forward. As you go on letting it out, one of two things will happen. Either the sail will reach the point where it cannot physically go out any farther, (in which case it should be pulled back in just enough to prevent chafe), or it will begin to luff. Luffing will be first noticeable along the leading edge of the sail, which is why this edge is called the *luff* of the sail.

If the sail begins to luff, you have let it out too far. Haul back in on the sheet until the luffing stops and that is the correct trim. Now F_t is as far forward as it can be and the sail is working most efficiently. If the sail never luffs it should be left out as far as possible, F_t will be pointing nearly straight ahead—a nice way to go!

For sailing close-hauled—as nearly into the wind as possible— the sail trimming procedure is somewhat different. In this case we do not know exactly what direction we will be able to sail until we try it. As the name suggests, sailing close-hauled means the sails are trimmed tightly in. For most sails this literally means as tight as possible, but in some cases there is an optimal position slightly short of that.

After the sails have been trimmed tight, the boat is *steered* closer and closer to the wind. This gradually reduces the angle of attack of all the sails at once. At the first sign of luffing the boat is steered back away from the wind until the sails are all full again. This is the best course that can be sailed to *windward*. It is now the helmsman's job to keep testing this optimal angle. He is ordered to steer *full-and-by,* which means that he must steer by the wind's direction, as close to it as possible, but keeping the sails full.

Usually when sailing close-hauled, the boat's destination is some-where upwind, closer to the wind's direction than can be sailed directly. To reach it she must sail close-hauled on one tack for a while, then turn and sail close-hauled on the other tack. This process of zigzagging to go upwind is known as *beating to wind-ward,* a truly descriptive term since sailing close-hauled to the wind also means punching into the waves that the wind is making. The overall effect is generally regarded as being toward the low end of the comfort scale!

The better the helmsman can keep the boat full-and-by, the more

FIG. 4-11

efficiently the destination will be reached. If he *pinches* and allows the sails to luff, the boat will go slower than she should, and make excessive leeway. On the other hand, if he steers farther away from the wind than is necessary to keep the sails full, more miles will have to be travelled to get there. It takes constant attention to sail efficiently to windward.

MANEUVERS

An important part of shiphandling is what must take place each time the boat in Figure 4-11 changes direction. As she travels the zigzag course, the wind comes first over one side of the boat and then the other. We say that she is first on the port tack, then the starboard tack, and so forth. At each "corner" the boat must be turned and the clews of all the sails shifted from one side of the boat to the other.

There are two ways the boat can turn in order to change tacks. In Figure 4-11 she changed tacks by turning first 90° to the left, then 90° to the right, etc. In Figure 4-12 she has accomplished the same result by turning 270° the opposite way each time. Although apparently less efficient, the latter is sometimes preferable, especially in larger vessels. The first maneuver is called *coming about,* and involves steering the bow of the boat through the *eye of the wind* (that is, for at least a moment the boat will point directly into the wind). The second method is called *jibing.* In this maneuver the stern of the boat is turned through the wind. There are many things to take into account when deciding whether to come about or jibe

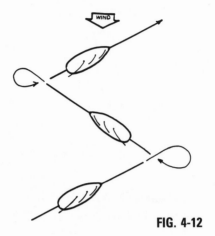

FIG. 4-12

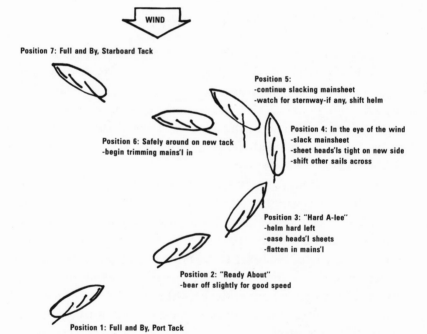

Position 7: Full and By, Starboard Tack

Position 5:
-continue slacking mainsheet
-watch for sternway-if any, shift helm

Position 6: Safely around on new tack
-begin trimming mains'l in

Position 4: In the eye of the wind
-slack mainsheet
-sheet heads'ls tight on new side
-shift other sails across

Position 3: "Hard A-lee"
-helm hard left
-ease heads'l sheets
-flatten in mains'l

Position 2: "Ready About"
-bear off slightly for good speed

Position 1: Full and By, Port Tack

FIG. 4-13

when the boat must change tacks. To make comparisons, we must look at what each maneuver entails.

Figure 4-13 shows the boat going through the sequence of steps necessary to come about from close-hauled on the port tack to close-hauled on the starboard tack. In position 1 she is full-and-by on the port tack; the wind is coming over the port side, the sails are sheeted to starboard. The crew is told to get ready for this maneuver by the command *"ready about."* Getting ready means seeing that the sheets of all the sails in use are clear and ready for handling, and that the helmsman is ready for the next command, which is *"hard a-lee."* (Note: this expression comes from when all ships were steered with tillers. A tiller is pushed to the lee side, or the downwind side, to turn the ship into the wind.) This command tells him to turn the wheel so the boat is turned hard toward the wind.

Now, if the helmsman has been steering full-and-by, we know that turning the boat any further toward the wind will cause the sails to luff and lose their drive. The force propelling the boat will cease, and the drag force of the wind against the luffing sails, masts, rigging and hull will soon bring the boat to a stop. If that happened of course the rudder would no longer steer the boat and we would say that she was *in irons*. This can be a predicament for the boat, embarrassing at best, and dangerous in some circumstances. What we are counting on to avoid getting stuck in irons is momentum. Before we start to come about we must have enough momentum to carry us through the eye of the wind and over onto the other tack where the sails can fill again and resume propelling us forward. Often the helmsman is told to *bear off* (steer away from the wind) slightly before going hard a-lee to get some extra speed as a sort of running start.

As soon as the boat begins to turn and the sails start luffing, it is important to complete the turn as quickly as possible. Remembering how strong a turning force the sails can provide suggests that we use them to facilitate the turning of the boat. At first we want to turn her toward the wind. Therefore we should have the CE as far aft as possible. To achieve that we would like more sail area aft and less forward. Our sail plan at present is balanced with CE only slightly aft of the CLR. One way to unbalance this in the desired

75

direction would be to reduce sail area forward. It is too cumbersome and time-consuming to actually strike sails for this, but it serves the same purpose to simply let their sheets go so that they luff and offer minimal resistance to the wind. So, at the same moment we go hard a-lee, we slack the sheets of the three heads'ls. As a result CE moves way aft producing a strong turning force on the boat in the direction we want.

In position 2 she is turning quickly under the combined influence of the rudder and the force of the mains'l unbalanced by heads'ls. In position 3 she is crossing the eye of the wind and the sails are completely luffing, so she is totally dependent on momentum. Assuming that she has enough speed she will make it on around. If not, and she stops before crossing the wind's eye, she will be in irons, have to fall back onto the port tack and start over.

Once through the wind's eye (position 4), the boat still has to continue turning until she is far enough *away* from the wind again so that her sails will fill on the new tack. By this time, most of her momentum will probably be spent and the rudder ineffective, so once again we must use the sails to turn the boat. This time, however, we want the opposite effect because we are trying to turn away from the wind, not into it. Where previously we had let the heads'ls luff to move CE aft, we now trim them tightly in to catch and fill with wind as soon as possible and pull the bow around downwind. At the same time, to get CE as far forward as we can, we slack the mainsheet out, allowing the mains'l to luff as long as needed. If this was not done, the mains'l would fill with wind and force the boat back up into the wind again.

The wind has carried the mains'l across the boat. The heads'ls were shifted and trimmed to the port side as she came through the eye. Any other sails that were set were likewise brought across as the boat went through the wind's eye, and trimmed for the new tack. As soon as she has turned far enough for them to fill, she starts to pick up speed and steerageway. Then the mains'l can be brought in and trimmed again for sailing close-hauled. The helmsman is ordered to steer full-and-by, and the maneuver is completed.

The other way to get from port tack to starboard tack is to turn the boat to the right, away from the wind, and jibe. Figure 4-14 shows the sequence of steps involved in jibing. There is no risk of getting into irons, losing headway or steerageway when jibing because the sails are working throughout the maneuver. If anything the boat will gain speed while jibing.

To begin turning the boat away from the wind, a combination of rudder effect and sail trim is needed as it was in coming about. Putting the rudder to the right will make her start to turn, but because her mains'l is trimmed in tight for sailing close-hauled, her

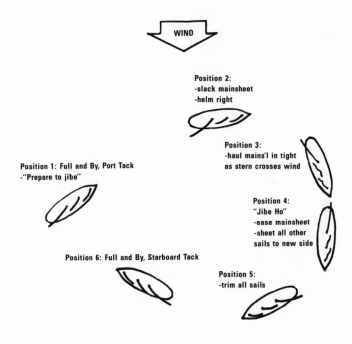

FIG. 4-14

CE is aft and she will not turn far before the force of the wind on the mains'l overpowers the rudder and makes her want to turn back toward the wind. The solution is to slack out the mainsheet, luffing the mains'l and shifting CE forward. Then she will head off easily.

As her heading approaches straight downwind (position 3), the mains'l will *blanket* the other sails ahead of it—that is, prevent the wind from filling them—and they will flap to and fro. This is a signal that the wind is nearly directly astern. It is a crucial signal to catch because if the wind crosses the stern and comes even slightly from the same side as the slacked-out mains'l, it will swing the mains'l violently to the other side of the boat with every likelihood of doing serious damage to people and/or gear.

Instead, what *must* happen before the wind crosses the stern is that we must haul the mains'l in. If the sheet is in as tight as it can be when the wind catches the other side of the sail, there is nowhere for it to swing. It will merely flip gently to the new side and the sheet can then be slacked out slowly. During or just after this critical moment, all the other sails, which are still well-blanketed, can be shifted to the new side and trimmed for sailing close-hauled. The helmsman steers the boat carefully up to full-and-by on the starboard tack, and the jibe is completed.

Whenever the boat must be turned from one tack to the other we must choose between coming about or jibing. The choice will depend many things, but in general, we would probably choose to jibe when—

- we have plenty of sea-room, enough for a 270° turn;
- the sea is rough and we are concerned that our momentum would not carry us through the eye of the wind if we tried to come about;
- it is windy and we want to avoid the wear and tear of luffing the sails and shaking the rig as we go through the eye;
- we are shorthanded, or do not want to call out extra hands to handle all the sails at once in coming about. In jibing, only the mains'l must be handled during the jibe, the others can be tended later.

On the other hand, we would prefer to come about when—

- in close quarters there may not be room to jibe, or we do not want to lose the ground between tacks that the 270° turn requires,
- conditions are smooth, speed is good, and we have plenty of hands on deck.

From this it should be apparent that a large sailing vessel at sea is likely to jibe more often than come about. Smaller vessels in confined and protected waters are more likely to come about.

It should also be apparent that whichever way we go, correct handling of the sails is vital to the success of the maneuver. The turning influence of the CE, whose position is determined by the selection and trim of the sails, is tremendous. In most cases it outweighs the effect of the rudder by a considerable amount. If a vessel loses her rudder she can be steered by sail trim alone, but if sails are not handled correctly no amount of rudder will turn her.

TO HEAVE-TO

One other important item of sail handling is the maneuver known as *heaving-to*. Heaving-to is bringing the boat to a stop at sea, and keeping her there. Unless the bottom can be reached with an anchor, there is no way to hold the boat in one precise spot at sea, but when she is hove-to her drift is reduced to a minimum. Furthermore, being hove-to is a safe and comfortable position for the boat relative to the wind and seas. Under reduced sail she can ride out heavy weather by heaving-to as long as she has enough sea-room to leeward.

FIG. 4-15

The procedure is to trim the sails so that their forces contradict one another and hold the boat in equilibrium at a steady angle to the

79

wind, but not moving forward. Figure 4-15 shows the schooner hove-to on the port tack. Her rudder is put over in the direction of the wind and kept there by lashing the wheel. Her mains'l is close-hauled and producing its normal force, which tries to propel the boat forward and turn her into the wind. The other sails are trimmed to the *wrong* side for this tack. They are said to be *aback,* or *backed.* This causes their F_t's to drive the boat backwards while trying to turn her away from the wind.

If the mains'l gets the upper hand, the boat begins to move forward. But that sail's turning effect plus the effect of the rudder make her turn toward the wind. Soon the mains'l will luff and lose its influence. At the same time the other backed sails are feeling the force of the wind more and more. When the mains'l luffs, they win out and push the boat backwards, turning her away from the wind again. Thus over a period of several minutes, the boat slowly oscillates back and forth, and her net progress is a slight drift downwind at an angle approximately as shown.

While she is hove-to she will look after herself. No steering is necessary, for as long as the sail plan is balanced fore and aft, she will maintain this orientation to the wind.

SUMMARY

These are the bare bones of shiphandling under sail. This is how it can be visualized in two dimensions on paper, where we can diagram the forces and discuss their effects. As with so many practical things, however, an intellectual understanding is only an aid. Real understanding comes only with real experience, when the forces are invisible but clearly felt and impossible to ignore: the tilt of the deck, hiss of water past the side when the sails are well-trimmed and drawing, the shake and thunder of a luffing jib, or the crash of a stack of dishes in the galley because we forgot to let the cook know we were coming about. . .

CHAPTER FIVE

The Diesel Engine

The modern sailing vessel has developed a great dependence upon auxiliary power. However much she uses the wind as a primary means of propulsion, by today's standards she will have to have an engine (or engines) to safely and efficiently fulfill her mission. Without auxiliary propulsion she may be unable to keep to a schedule, or unable to maneuver into a berth without expensive assistance. Without a generator she will not have lights, radios, radar, or the benefit of electronic navigation. Increasingly, the diesel has become the auxiliary engine of choice for vessels large and small.

The diesel engine has earned a good reputation for performance at sea, an environment which is hostile to high precision technology due to the corrosiveness of salt water. The diesel's success aboard ship is due to its fundamental simplicity, which means that there is relatively little that can go wrong with it. The kinds of problems that may occur are usually possible to diagnose and repair at sea. With an understanding of the basic process whereby the diesel converts fuel into mechanical energy, and with some deductive reasoning, it is possible for anyone to diagnose 90 percent of the problems that are likely to bother a diesel. Most of these problems can be remedied either by common sense or by simple replacement of parts.

The intent of this chapter is not to train diesel technicians but to describe the engine in a way which will enable you to think logically about the engine you are operating and, when problems arise, to think deductively from the symptoms to the cause. We will start by briefly putting the diesel in context: seeing where it fits historically as an engine, prime mover, doer of work.

At first it was just our own arms and backs doing all the world's work. We learned to use tools and got a mechanical advantage on things, but we ourselves were the only source of power. Then we persuaded some animals to hold still long enough so that we could hitch a load to them, and we had another source of power. When we jumped on a log and spread a sail we'd discovered yet another—the wind. Soon there were windmills, and moving water was put to work by water wheels.

All of these—people, animals, sails, water wheels, etc.—are prime movers, converting some form of available energy into a mechanical force that can do work. Heat is a form of energy that has been available to us from the beginning, but only relatively recently did we discover how to convert it into a mechanical force. The diesel is a modern *heat engine* which does this.

HERO'S AEOLIPILE   **FIG. 5-1**

The earliest recorded evidence of a heat engine is a drawing of a device called an aeolipile (Figure 5-1) conceived by Hero of Alexandria in 75 B.C., and probably never built. Regardless of the fact that it is shown doing nothing more useful than imparting a feeling of satisfaction to its creator, it nevertheless could have converted heat from burning fuel into a mechanical force (rotation of the sphere) capable of doing some work. It is a heat engine, and the means by which it converts heat into a force is the same as is found in the diesel: namely through *pressure*. In the aeolipile the heat energy is used to boil water which expands, becoming steam. Since it is in a confined space, this expansion creates pressure. The steam is allowed to escape through the two jets, and as it does Newton reminds us that for every action there is an equal and opposite reaction, so the escaping steam would have sent the jets forcibly backwards like a deflating balloon on the loose, and the sphere would have spun around. There it is: heat energy converted to mechanical energy through the medium of a pressure change in a fluid . . . a concept to keep in mind.

BRANCA'S STEAM TURBINE

FIG. 5-2

Several hundred years later a page from Mr. Branca's notebook (Figure 5-2) shows us a heat engine with a practical purpose imagined, although it is again doubtful whether in reality it would have saved the baker much trouble. Once again it is the pressure of water changed to steam which enables the heat energy to be expressed as a force. In this case, however, the escaping steam strikes the blades of the turbine (paddle wheel) delivering energy through *impact* rather than *reaction*.

Finally, in 1698 we come upon a breakthrough—the first heat engine that was built and put to practical use. In response to the need to remove water from underground coal mines, much creative thinking went into various ways of pumping water at this time. Thomas Savery designed, built and patented a "fire engine" (as he called it) for raising water more easily and efficiently than by driving teams of horses hitched to mechanical pumps. His engine did not have the moving parts that we tend to associate with an engine but it did convert heat into mechanical work (Figure 5-3).

Water was boiled in a container and the steam was led into a chamber from the bottom of which a pipe went down into the water in the mine. When the chamber was full of steam all openings to the chamber were closed except the pipe to the mine. Now when water changes from a liquid to a vapor it expands 1600 times, and conversely when it condenses back to a liquid it contracts the same amount. So as the steam in the chamber cooled it condensed and contracted, creating a vacuum which sucked water up the pipe from the mine nearly filling the chamber. The work was done and the energy that did it was the heat which had expanded the water into steam. All that remained to be done was to close a valve in the mine-pipe and open a drain valve to empty the chamber and the process could begin again.

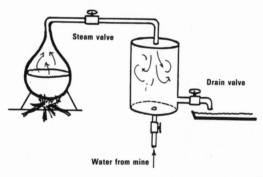

Steam valve

Drain valve

Water from mine

FIG. 5-3

A man was needed to open and close the valves in sequence, and another to stoke the fire and fill the boiler now and then, but the horses could go back to the field. Notice once again a fluid medium—water/steam—converts the energy:

$$\text{heat} \rightarrow \text{pressure} \rightarrow \text{mechanical force}$$

Notice, too, that it is a cyclical process at work, a sequence of events repeated over and over, and that these events are regulated by *valves*. All of these are important elements of the diesel engine also.

Savery's fire engine was a great success and improvements came rapidly. By 1715, the same concept was the basis of a more sophisticated pumping engine patented by Thomas Newcommen. His engine featured some important developments (Figure 5-4). Instead of condensing the steam in a chamber directly piped to the mine, Newcommen's engine condensed the steam in a *cylinder* which was fitted at its top end with a *piston*, free to move up and down. As the steam condensed forming a vacuum in the cylinder, the piston was forced down by the atmospheric pressure above it. This force tipped the pivoted beam to which the piston was attached, and that in turn pulled up on the pump rod, raising water from the mine. The condensation of the steam was hastened by injecting a spray of cold water into the cylinder once it was full of steam. The several valves which had to be operated over and over in sequence were arranged to be self-acting, thanks — so the story goes — to the creative laziness of the boy whose job it was to tend them. This engine could therefore run itself: the weight of the pump rod would tip the beam and pull the piston up, drawing steam into the cylinder from the boiler. When it reached the top a string pulled the steam valve closed and the water spray valve open. The steam condensed quickly, sucking the piston down and lifting water from the mine. When the piston reached the bottom of its stroke another string reversed the valves and the cycle would repeat.

A typical Newcommen engine had a cylinder three feet in diameter, its piston moved through a nine-foot stroke, and it operated at a rate of about 15 strokes per minute. It is said to have done in 48 hours the work that had previously required 50 men and 20 horses working 24 hours a day for a week!

The advent of the piston and cylinder meant that we now had a mechanically reciprocating piston rod with the potential for driving other things besides pumps. Unfortunately, however, most of the work that needed doing required a rotating force (millstones,

THOMAS NEWCOMMEN'S PUMPING ENGINE

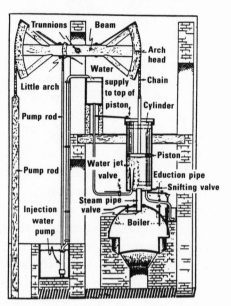

FIG. 5-4

lathes, saws, wheels, etc.) and it was curiously not obvious to our ancestors how a reciprocating motion could be converted into a rotating one. Curious because the opposite concept was well understood and used, as in Branca's pounding machine and many pumping devices, where a rotating force from a windmill or water wheel was converted to a reciprocating motion through the use of a *crank* (Figure 5-5).

What was needed was recognition of how to employ a *flywheel* to convert intermittent reciprocating pushes on a crank into a smooth rotation. Figure 5-5 shows a *crankshaft,* which can rotate, and a *connecting rod,* which reciprocates. If we push or pull on the connecting rod the shaft will turn this way and that, and in between it will stop. If we attach a flywheel to the shaft, however, the mass of the flywheel will act as an energy storer. Now when we push on the

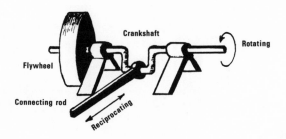

FIG. 5-5

connecting rod some of the energy of the push is stored in the flywheel as momentum. When the push ends at the end of a stroke the momentum of the flywheel keeps the shaft rotating in the same direction until the crank reaches a position for another push. Thus, although the energy is delivered intermittently to the crankshaft the flywheel evens it out and the shaft rotates smoothly. Here is rotating power ready to grind grain, saw lumber . . . or turn a propeller.

THE RECIPROCATING STEAM ENGINE

Throughout the 19th century the *reciprocating steam engine* evolved from these first pumping engines to become the number one source of power for industry and transportation. It continued as such until well into this century when it has been gradually replaced by the more efficient steam turbine engine, and the *internal combustion* engines: gasoline and diesel.

As was the case with the earlier steam engines, this is an *external combustion* heat engine. The heat is produced by burning fuel in the furnace of a boiler outside the engine. It acts on a working fluid—water—which expands into steam and is piped to the engine. The heart of the engine is its cylinder and piston. Here in this closed chamber, changes in pressure are felt as a mechanical force by the piston and reciprocating motion results. All the rest of the engine's parts are either to convert the reciprocating motion to rotary, or to make the engine self-acting. We will follow the engine in Figure 5-6 through a complete cycle and see how it all works together.

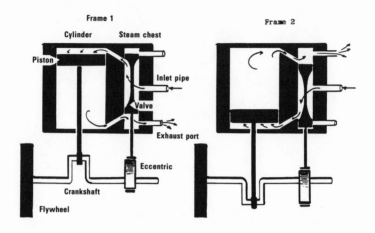

FIG. 5-6

In Frame 1 steam enters the *steam chest* from the boiler through the inlet pipe. Due to the position of the *valve* at this moment the only place the steam can go is through the passage into the top of the *cylinder*. Therefore, its pressure forces the piston down. The piston rod and connecting rod carry this push to the crank on the crankshaft and start it rotating. The attached flywheel absorbs some of this push and stores it as rotating momentum.

In addition to the crank and flywheel on the crankshaft, there is an off-center disc called an *eccentric*. As this rotates it imparts a reciprocating motion to the strap and rod which follow it. The rod is attached to the valve, so that as the crankshaft turns, the valve is moved up and down. When the valve moves down (Frame 2) the steam is redirected from the top of the cylinder to the bottom, underneath the piston. The momentum of the flywheel carries the crank past the bottom, and now the steam pushing up on the piston from below causes a *pull* on the crank, imparting more force to the crankshaft's rotation. When the piston nears the top the valve is changed again and the process repeats.

Notice that in addition to directing the incoming steam, the valve also provides a way for the spent steam to leave the cylinder. In Frame 1 as the piston is being pushed down, the space below the piston is open to the atmosphere via an *exhaust port*. Spent steam is pushed out. In Frame 2 the space above the piston is similarly open.

So here is a fairly simple means of converting heat to a rotating force which can be put to work. Inefficiencies abound, of course. Heat losses in the boiler and in the transport of steam to the engine, heat lost in the engine itself, friction of moving parts, energy remaining in the spent steam exhausted to the atmosphere—all these represent inefficiencies.

We have looked at a single cylinder, double-acting, noncondensing engine. In its heyday in the early 20th century, the reciprocating steam engine was more commonly a double- or triple-expansion, condensing type engine. This meant that it had two or three cylinders side by side turning cranks on the same crankshaft. The cylinders were of different diameters. The high pressure steam straight from the boiler went first to the smallest cylinder. When it was exhausted from that one it was still under pressure, though somewhat reduced, so it was sent to the next larger cylinder where it delivered more of its energy to that piston. At still less pressure, the exhaust steam from this cylinder went to the largest one, after which it had very little pressure left. Then instead of being vented to the atmosphere, it was led to a condenser, changed into water again, and pumped back into the boiler for re-use. These features were not only energy efficient, but also saved fresh water, which was important on a ship with limited tank capacity.

This was the work-horse of the early 20th century, providing the motive power for ships, trains, mills, and factories. Through World War II the navies and merchant fleets of the world were powered primarily by triple-expansion steam engines, but a competitor was appearing on the scene. In 1898 Rudolf Diesel successfully demonstrated his invention of an internal combustion engine which was to prove more efficient and versatile than the steam engine in all but the largest applications such as large ships and power plants. In those situations the steam turbine engine is still competitive with the diesel in efficiency.

THE DIESEL ENGINE

The diesel is a heat engine. Like the steam engine, the diesel converts heat into rotating mechanical power through the medium of a *working fluid,* but this time the fluid is air.

Boyle's laws relate the temperature, pressure, and volume of a gas, and tell us that if you compress a gas its pressure and its temperature will rise, and conversely if it is allowed to expand they drop. Picture a simple cylinder, piston, connecting rod, and crankshaft with flywheel as shown in Figure 5-7.

If we hung a weight on the flywheel as shown so that it turned half a turn to position 2, the piston would move up, compressing the air in the cylinder. If the weight were just heavy enough to do this, its effort would have been converted to potential energy in the form of a) higher pressure and b) higher temperature in the cylinder.

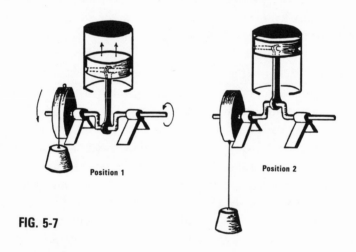

Position 1

Position 2

FIG. 5-7

Assuming an ideal situation with no friction, heat, or pressure losses, this would be exactly enough energy to drive the piston down again and lift the weight back up to its original height. In other words, the air in the cylinder would undergo a cycle: the piston does a certain amount of work on the air, then the air returns

FIG. 5-8

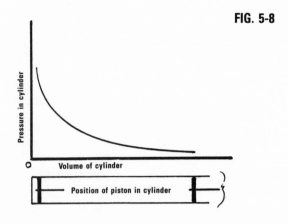

FIG. 5-9

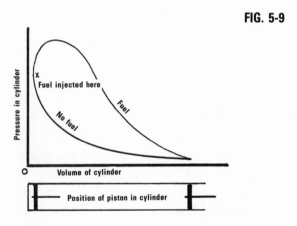

the same amount of work to the piston. Or: energy in equals energy out. A graph of pressure vs. volume for the cylinder undergoing this cycle would look like Figure 5-8.

This is not an engine—yet. There is no energy surplus anywhere that could be used to do any work.

However, if we add to this balanced cycle an extra input of energy at some point, we can expect an equal output of energy, perhaps in a different form, at some other point. If, for example, at the point on the graph in Figure 5-8 where the piston is all the way up and pressure is greatest, we were to add some heat energy by burning fuel *in the cylinder,* the compressed and already hot air would be heated still hotter. According to Boyle, heating a gas increases its pressure if volume is constant, so the pressure in the cylinder would be made higher than before, as shown by the graph in Figure 5-9.

Higher pressure means greater force on the piston, so it would be pushed down extra hard—the extra amount being equivalent to the amount of heat added by burning the fuel. This extra is represented on the graph by the area between the curve for "no fuel" and the curve for "fuel." It represents an energy input which will show up at the crankshaft as an output of mechanical energy available to go to work. Now we have a true engine, converting energy from heat to a mechanical force.

This is the basis of the diesel engine. In practice, this basic cycle is achieved in one of two ways. Since both are in common use on boats, we will look at each.

THE FOUR-STROKE CYCLE

Figure 5-10 illustrates what is called a *four-stroke cycle*. Each movement of the piston up or down is a stroke. When an engine is running the cycle is occurring over and over continuously, so any stroke can be used as a starting point for discussion. We will jump in at the beginning of a *power stroke* (Frame 1). Fuel is being burned in the cylinder, heating air and raising its pressure. The piston is driven down, pushing the crank, turning the crankshaft and flywheel, and let's say turning the propeller of our boat. The flywheel stores much of the energy of the push as momentum, so that when the piston reaches the bottom of the power stroke, it keeps the crankshaft turning. This means that next the piston will come back up, pushed by the crank. The cylinder is full of exhaust gases, however, by-products of the combustion that just took place, and if the piston is to rise in the cylinder these gases must be allowed to escape. Therefore, an opening is made in the *cylinder head* by a valve which allows the exhaust gas to be pushed out by the rising piston. This is the *exhaust stroke* (Frame 2).

In Frame 3, the piston has reached the top, the exhaust has been expelled, and the exhaust valve closes. The flywheel's momentum

FIG. 5-10

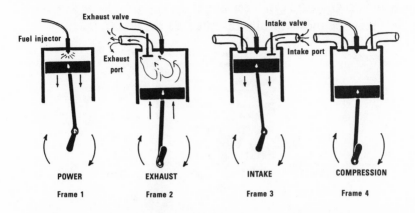

continues to turn the crankshaft and the piston is pulled downward by the crank. Now a second valve opens in the top of the cylinder so that the descending piston draws in a cylinderful of fresh air. This is the *intake stroke*. Finally, in Frame 4 both valves are closed and the piston, pushed up once more by the momentum of the flywheel, compresses the fresh air in the cylinder. As a result of this *compression stroke*, the temperature of the air rises — so much that at the top of the compression stroke it is heated well above the kindling temperature of diesel fuel. It is into this very hot air that the fuel is injected — sprayed — by a powerful pump through an *injector*. The heat ignites it, and another power strokes occurs, beginning the cycle anew.

As can be seen in a four-stroke engine, the crankshaft must make two revolutions to produce one power stroke. This makes the flywheel essential to absorb enough energy from each power stroke to sustain the rotation through the subsequent exhaust, intake, and compression strokes. This is especially important in a single-cylinder engine. If the engine has two or more cylinders, they are arranged to fire alternately (i.e., their cycles are staggered) and the need for a flywheel is less.

Just as with the steam engine, we see that the diesel engine's cycle is directed by the sequential opening and closing of valves. We identified an exhaust valve, an intake valve, and also an injector, through which fuel entered the cylinder. These must each perform their function at the right time in relation to the piston's movement up and down in the cylinder, and, if the engine is to be self-acting, they must be mechanically operated by the engine itself.

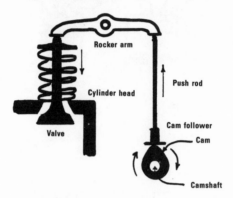

FIG. 5-11

Exhaust and intake valves are most commonly of the type shown in Figure 5-11. They are held closed by springs and must be pushed open at the appropriate time. This is done by a *rocker-arm* and *push-rod* arrangement as shown, which gets its impetus from a revolving *cam*. A cam, like the steam engine's eccentric, is a device for changing rotary motion to linear motion. A *follower* rides on the cam and every time the cam's lobe comes around the follower is moved up and down. When the follower is connected to the push-rod/rocker-arm/valve assembly, the cam will control the opening and closing of the valve. All that remains is to link the rotation of the cam to the movement of the piston so that the valve will be opened at the right moment in the four-stroke sequence. This is done by placing the cams—one for each valve—on a *cam shaft* which is turned by the crankshaft either through gears or by a chain drive, as is pictured in Figure 5-12.

Since a given valve event happens once for every two revolutions of the crankshaft in a four-stroke engine, the cam shaft must be turned half as fast as the crankshaft. Therefore the gear ratio or sprocket ratio of the chain drive must be 2:1.

In Figure 5-12 there are three cams on the cam shaft. There is one each for the exhaust and intake valves, and the third is for the fuel

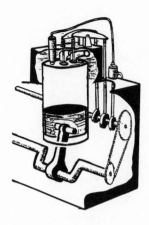

FIG. 5-12

pump. Once every four strokes fuel must be injected into the cylinder for a power stroke. The pump which does this is activated by this third cam. At the right moment this cam's follower moves a piston in the fuel pump which forces fuel through a pipe to the injector and it is sprayed into the cylinder.

Thus the mechanism of the cam shaft causes all the events of the cycle to happen in the proper order and at the right instant, and the engine, *once started,* is able to run itself.

THE TWO-STROKE CYCLE

The basic diesel cycle can also be accomplished in two strokes. Figure 5-13 illustrates the two-stroke cycle.

In Frame 1, the power stroke is similar to what we saw in the four-stroke engine. When the piston approaches the bottom of its travel, however, there is a difference. It uncovers openings called *ports* in the sides of the cylinder. From one side fresh air is forced in by a blower. This replaces the exhaust gases, blowing them out the other side. As the piston rises again, closing off the ports, clean fresh air is trapped in the cylinder. It is compressed by the rising piston, and ready for another injection of fuel as the piston reaches the top.

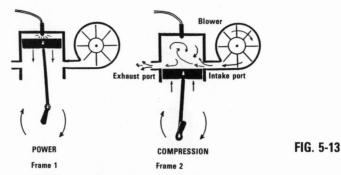

POWER
Frame 1

COMPRESSION
Frame 2

FIG. 5-13

This system has no need for valves (although some two-stroke engines do have them in addition to ports) and has a power stroke for every revolution of the crankshaft. This might suggest that for the same size engine a two-stroke cycle would produce twice the power that a four-stroke cycle would. Ideally that would be the case, but a major limitation of the two-stroke is the difficulty of effecting a complete exchange of exhaust for fresh air in the brief moment that the piston is down. In addition, the need for a blower offsets the advantage of not having valves and detracts from its efficiency. There are many other bases for comparison between the two, and each type of engine has its advocates, but both are equally commonplace at present.

Without going into unnecessary detail, it is worthwhile to point out briefly how the gasoline engine differs from the diesel. Both are internal combustion engines. The diesel is known as a *compression ignition* engine. That is because the fuel is ignited by the heat of the compressed air in the cylinder when it is injected. The gasoline engine is a *spark ignition* engine. Whereas the diesel intakes and compresses pure fresh air, the gasoline engine intakes a mixture of air and vaporized gasoline. This mixture is provided and regulated by the *carburetor*. In the compression stroke it is compressed, but not to the point that it ignites. An electric spark made by the *spark plug* is needed to ignite the mixture. Therefore the gasoline engine must have a source of electricity—a battery or magneto—to supply the spark. Because the compression ratio of a gasoline engine is much lower than that of a diesel, the engine need not be as strong and can be lighter in weight for a given horsepower. This is a big reason why the gasoline engine has dominated the automobile and airplane industry for so long. Diesels have been more popular at sea where weight is not so critical, and where carburetors and electrical systems are hard to maintain.

DIESEL ENGINE SYSTEMS

Once the basic cycles are understood you may wonder why the average engine is so complicated-looking. A diesel engine ought to appear fairly simple: a crankshaft with flywheel and crank, a connecting rod, a piston moving in a cylinder, some valves (or ports) and an injector in the cylinder head, and—if valves—then a cam shaft and linkage to move the valves. In actuality, of the above mentioned parts only the flywheel and the injector are likely to be visible. The rest of these parts are enclosed in the *block* and some disassembly is necessary to see them. Most of what you do see when you look at an engine is an array of pipes, hoses, pumps, filters, and wires—all parts belonging to the several systems which support the engine's basic cycle. These are:

- the fuel system
- the lubrication system
- the cooling system
- the starting system

Each of these is vital to the engine's health. A failure within one of these systems will likely mean that the engine will not run, and nine times out of ten if the engine is malfunctioning the problem will be found in one of the systems and not in the basic cycle. We will therefore look at the purpose of each system, what it consists of, how it is monitored, and what would happen if it failed. The best diagnostic approach to a sick engine is to be able to trace out each of its systems.

THE FUEL SYSTEM

The purpose of the fuel system is to supply the right amount of fuel at the right moment to each cylinder. It includes everything from

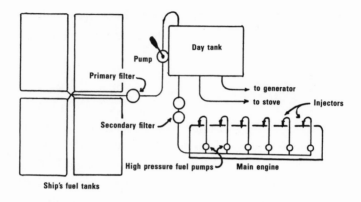

FIG. 5-14

the boat's fuel tanks to the injector. Figure 5-14 is a diagram of a typical boats's fuel system.

In a large ship, fuel may be carried in many tanks throughout the ship. By valves and piping, the engineer can select from which tank to draw fuel. Since these tanks are apt to hold upwards of 1,000 gallons, it is usual practice to bring only a small amount of fuel at a time into the engine room by periodically filling a *day tank*. Then if there were a fire or other accident in the engine room there would not be a large amount of fuel present. The day tank is kept full either by a hand pump or a pump driven by the engine. From the day tank, fuel lines run to the engines, the stove, the furnace, and any other consumers. In smaller boats the various consumers may be piped directly to the main tank.

As the fuel is moved by pumps from the tanks to the engine it is led through several *filters* of increasing fineness. This is to ensure that water (from condensation in the tanks) and dirt (rust, grit, etc.) do not enter the delicate high-pressure pumps and injectors. These are the most sensitive parts of a diesel engine—the injector tip has almost microscopically small holes in it through which the fuel is sprayed. If they clog, the fuel may dribble and not burn properly, or may be stopped completely. Filters are canisters with replaceable paper elements which must be serviced (replaced) regularly or they will clog and stop the fuel. A common cause of loss of power or engine failure is clogged fuel filters.

The fuel is delivered to the high-pressure fuel pump either by gravity from the tank or by a low pressure fuel pump driven by the engine through a mechanical connection to the crankshaft or cam shaft, so that whenever the engine runs, fuel is pumped. The high-pressure fuel pump, as we have already seen, is driven by a third cam, timed with the other two, to the basic cycle. This pump must push the fuel hard enough so that it will enter the cylinder against the pressure of the air at the end of the compression stroke. Moreover, it must pump just the right *amount* of fuel to run the engine at the speed desired. The more fuel it injects, the faster the engine will run. In this function the fuel pump is regulated by a centrifugal device called a *governor*. The governor senses and controls the engine's speed. The operator sets the governor to the desired speed and the governor adjusts the fuel pump to maintain that speed. If an extra load is placed on the engine, which would tend to slow it down, the governor responds by making the fuel pump pump more fuel on each power stroke, thus bringing the speed back up. The linkage between the governor and the fuel pump is called the *rack*. In a multi-cylinder engine one governor is tied to the fuel pumps for each cylinder by a rack running the length of the engine.

The last item in the fuel system is the injector, which is essentially a very precise nozzle designed to atomize the fuel as it enters the cylinder. This helps ensure even and complete burning of the fuel, which is important to the efficiency of the engine. Worn and dirty injectors make for lost power, smoky exhaust, and eventually an engine that will not run.

Monitoring the fuel system means ensuring that there is fuel in the tanks supplying the engine, and then seeing that it is getting through the lines and filters to the pumps. Some systems are equipped with pressure gauges in the fuel lines to show if fuel is being pumped at correct pressures.

THE LUBRICATION SYSTEM

Lubrication is the business of reducing friction between moving parts. An engine is full of parts moving against one another. Without lubrication they would quickly heat up and destroy each other.

Lubricants such as oil and grease serve to separate, or at least minimize the metal-to-metal contact between parts, thus reducing friction.

When mechanical parts move together they form what is called a *bearing*. Two common types of bearings are (1) slipper bearings, where parts slide against each other, and (2) journal bearings, where one part (the shaft) rotates inside another (the journal), (Figure 5-15).

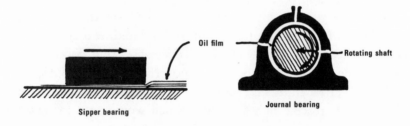

FIG. 5-15

Lubricants come in different grades according to their viscosity. The correct choice of viscosity depends on the speed at which the bearing surfaces are moving and how much load or pressure there is pressing them together. The higher the speed and the lighter the load the thinner the oil can be. Heavy, slow-moving parts may require grease to keep them apart.

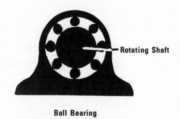

FIG. 5-16

In the typical engine there are many of both types of bearings. The piston sliding in the cylinder is a slipper bearing; the crank shaft rotates in its journal bearings.

Finally, in many high-speed, light-load situations, ball- or roller-bearings are used (Figure 5-16). The balls or rollers between the shaft and the outer ring reduce *surface contact* to *point contact,* eliminating much friction. These also require lubrication or the parts will wear quickly.

Every bearing in the engine must be continually lubricated and this is usually accomplished in one of two ways.

Wet Sump Lubrication

A sump is the enclosed space at the bottom of an engine below the crankshaft. All the main parts of the engine from the piston down are within the open space above this. It is filled with a supply of oil to a level such that the crank will dip into it as it turns. This action splashes oil throughout the space, continuously lubricating the crankshaft, cam shaft, cams and followers, timing gears, and cylinder walls. The only parts which cannot be reached this way are those above the piston—the valves, rocker arms, and push rods. They are lubricated by means of an oil pump which sends oil from the sump through piping to these bearings. From the bearings it returns to the sump to be recirculated.

Dry Sump Lubrication

In large engines, where it would be impractical to fill the sump with oil, a supply of oil is held in a tank near the engine. Pumps and piping deliver it to all the bearing surfaces in the engine. It drips down, collects in the sump, and then is pumped by another pump back to the tank.

In both arrangements all the oil is continuously circulated and in the process is sent through *oil filters* and an *oil cooler.* As it lubricates, the oil carries off minute particles of metal, carbon, and other grit. Filtering removes these abrasive impurities. It also carries heat away from the cylinder area of the engine, and if it was not cooled it would become hot enough to break down chemically, losing its viscosity and its ability to lubricate. An oil cooler is a *heat exchanger* in which the oil flows through a network of tubes surrounded by a circulation of cool water. Heat transfers from the

WET SUMP LUBRICATION

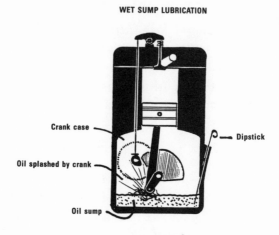

FIG. 5-17

oil to the water—normally seawater—which is pumped back over-board taking the heat with it. This requires a water pump driven by the engine.

Lubrication is so vital that an engine will not run more than a minute or two without it. It is therefore very important to monitor the lubrication system closely. This begins with being certain that there is the requisite amount of oil in the system (sump or tank) before starting the engine. Once it is running, an oil pressure gauge shows the pressure of the oil being pumped to the bearings. This pressure is only correct over a small range for a given engine. Too low a pressure would suggest that the pump was not working, or a pipe was broken, or that the oil supply was low. An abnormally high pressure, on the other hand, might mean that the circulation was obstructed, perhaps by a clogged filter. In either case, oil would not be getting to the bearings and continued running of the engine would be destructive. Most engines are equipped with alarms so that the operator is alerted immediately if the pressure varies from normal. Good practice with a running engine is to check the oil pressure gauge frequently.

THE COOLING SYSTEM

If a heat engine were perfectly efficient, all the heat energy from combustion would be converted to mechanical energy, there would be no friction between the moving parts, and the engine would not get hot. Certainly this is a goal, but even in the best of engines a large proportion of the fuel's energy is lost as heat which either escapes with the exhaust gases, or is absorbed by the metal of the engine. If this absorbed heat were not removed it would build up until the oil broke down and the metal parts melted. Therefore the engine must be cooled while it is running. The simplest cooling system is a flow of air past the cylinder and cylinder head in such a way that the heat is transferred to the air. Motorcycles, lawn-mowers, and chainsaws, for example, are cooled in this way. Typically, an air-cooled engine will have metal fins surrounding the cylinders to facilitate the transfer of heat to the air.

Air-cooling is only possible for small engines in installations where there is plenty of air exchange. Aboard a boat an engine mounted on deck could be air-cooled, but one installed below deck would have to be water-cooled. A water-cooled engine is designed and built with voids and passages in the block surrounding the cylinder, through which water or a coolant is circulated. Heat is picked up by the coolant which is pumped from the engine to a heat exchanger. There, in the same way that the oil was cooled, the coolant loses its heat to a separate circulation of sea water, and then is returned to the engine. The hot seawater is pumped overboard (Figure 5-18).

These two circulations each require a pump to drive them, adding two more to the list of pumps which the engine must drive to sustain its operation. Each of these circulations must also be monitored. The coolant circulates in a closed loop which includes a *header tank* where a supply of coolant must be maintained. The seawater circulation must be kept free of debris which might clog the pump or heat exchanger. A strainer is always fitted where the water is piped in through the hull, and this must be checked regularly.

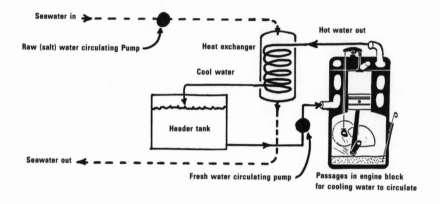

FIG. 5-18

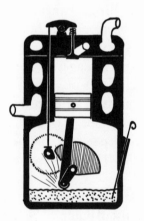

Any malfunction of the cooling system will result in the engine overheating, so a careful watch must be kept on thermometers showing the temperature of the coolant as it leaves the engine. These thermometers are often connected to an alarm which will signal any abnormal temperature.

STARTING SYSTEMS

When we discussed the basic cycle of the diesel we assumed the engine was already running. Each stroke of the cycle assumed that the preceding one had taken place, so how did it start?

An outside force is required to initiate the process—to rotate the crankshaft. Once the piston has been driven through an intake stroke and a compression stroke, the engine can "fire" and begin to run itself. Various sources of power are used to "turn over" an engine to start it.

Hand Starting

The simplest starting system is a removable crank fitted to the end of the crankshaft so that a person can rotate the crankshaft by hand. Although simple, this is difficult to do because of the force required to compress the air in the cylinder during the compression stroke. Therefore hand-cranking engines are usually equipped with a *compression release mechanism,* which keeps the exhaust valve open. This prevents compression from taking place and makes it relatively easy to get the crankshaft and flywheel spinning. When there is good momentum in the flywheel the exhaust valve is allowed to close, compression occurs—made easier by the flywheel—and the engine starts.

Electric Starting

On larger engines a mechanical means of starting must be used. Most commonly this is an electric starter. This is a powerful electric motor which, when turned on, engages the flywheel through gears and rotates it until the engine starts. Of course, a source of electricity to run the motor must be at hand, and this is normally in the form of a storage battery. To recharge the battery after starting there must be a generator—driven by the engine—and the circuitry to regulate the charging process. As suggested earlier, electrical systems are often difficult to maintain at sea chiefly due to corrosion, and they are apt to be a source of problems aboard ship.

These systems have added a lot of complexity to the basic, simple, two- or four-stroke diesel cycle. Each system adds pumps, heat exchangers, pipes, generators, etc., all of which make energy demands on the engine and reduce its overall efficiency. What is gained, on the other hand, is an engine which is essentially self-tending, managing its fuel supply, its lubrication needs, and cooling functions with a minimum of participation by the operator. The engineer's role is primarily to monitor the systems, and carry out preventive maintainance to reduce the chances of something wearing out, clogging up, or rusting away.

Aside from the gauges and alarms that report on various aspects of the engine's "health," the *sound, feel,* and even *smell* of the engine will reveal a lot about how it is doing to a person who has become familiar with it. Once accustomed to the normal rhythm of all an engine's parts in action, one notices the least change in its sound, and is compelled to investigate.

The only part of an engine that should be too hot to touch is where the exhaust leaves the engine. Anywhere else will be warm to very warm, but if it is *hot* it probably indicates a problem with the lubrication or cooling system. An overheated engine will smell hot from burning paint and boiling coolant. Exhaust leaks and fuel leaks have their own smells.

If something is not right the engine should be stopped and the symptoms examined until the cause is found. If completely baffled, start from scratch and remember that a diesel *must* have three things to run: (1) fuel, (2) air, and (3) compression to get the air hot enough to burn the fuel. If those items are present and in good shape then the systems should be checked through in detail with the symptoms in mind, and remembering that in many ways the systems affect each other.

A good example I once saw of this was a six-cylinder diesel which inexplicably began to overheat in its first three cylinders and run abnormally cool in the last three. Temperature symptoms suggested first a problem with the cooling system, and then possibly the lubrication system. Thorough checks revealed nothing wrong with either. Finally it was discovered that the fuel filters were partially clogged with sludge and only a small amount of fuel was getting to the engine. The governor, set for full speed, was trying to keep the engine up to speed by opening the fuel pumps farther and farther. There was only enough fuel coming through for the first three cylinders which were therefore trying to do the work of six and consequently overheating while the others were not firing at all. Once the filters were changed all ran normally again.

Different diesels will look different on first encounter, but if you begin by sorting what you see into parts belonging to this or that system, you can quickly find your way around and make sense of it all. It is a great satisfaction to understand even generally what is going on inside an engine, and when you are dependent on one at sea it is good to know that it nearly always responds to common sense!

CHAPTER SIX

Shiphandling Under Power

Having seen in the last chapter how the diesel engine converts fuel into mechanical energy, we will now look at how that energy is used to propel the boat. First we must see how the rotating force of the engine is converted to a propelling force on the boat's hull by means of the *drive train,* and then we will discuss how the boat is maneuvered using this force.

Installed inside the boat is a diesel engine, and outside the hull at the stern is a propeller. The parts that connect the two constitute what is called the drive train. There are as many different variations of drive trains as there are boats and engines but in general certain parts will always be present (Figure 6-1).

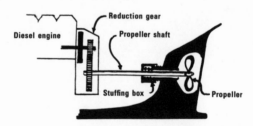

FIG. 6-1

The rotation of the crankshaft must be joined to the propeller and this is accomplished by a *propeller shaft.* The propeller shaft may be in one piece or in several, depending on the distance it must span. It is supported at appropriate intervals in its run by *shaft bearings*. The propeller is attached to its after end, and at its forward end it either directly or indirectly connects to the engine's crankshaft.

At some point it must pass through the hull of the boat, and since this is below the waterline there must be an arrangement made to keep water from getting in at this point. This is done by means of the *stern tube* and *stuffing box*. Immediately forward of the propeller is a bearing, and then the shaft enters the hull through the stern tube which is made watertight with the skin of the hull. Where the shaft leaves this tube inside the hull there is the stuffing box. This is a gland, filled with *packing* and fitted with a threaded nut which is tightened, squeezing the packing around the shaft. The packing is impregnated with a lubricant so that the shaft is able to rotate within it. This prevents water from getting past, although a slight drip is usually permitted to seep through to prevent the packing from heating up. When the boat is under power the stuffing box must be periodically checked to see that the drip is present but not excessive, and that the gland is not overheating.

Before connecting the forward end of the propeller shaft to the engine's crankshaft, there are two things which must be considered. First, if the boat is to be able to be propelled astern as well as ahead, we may need to provide a *reverse gear* and *clutch*. Second, the optimum speed of rotation for the engine is usually not the same as that for the propeller. This discrepancy is resolved by the *reduction gear*.

Most small and medium size diesels are made to rotate in just one direction. The cams for the valves and fuel pumps are timed for that rotation. If it is desired to have the option of turning the propeller either way, then a reverse gear is fitted to the engine. By means of a gear train and clutch, the reverse gear enables the operator to choose one rotation or the other, or disengage the engine from the propeller shaft entirely, so that the engine is running but the propeller does not turn. The controls for this are normally located on deck and handled by the operator.

Large ships sometimes avoid the need for a reverse gear by an arrangement whereby the engine itself rotates either way. This necessitates having two cams instead of one for each valve and fuel pump such that one is timed for one rotation and the other for the opposite rotation. They are placed side by side on the cam shaft and the whole cam shaft is moved longitudinally to bring one or the other set of cams into action. The engine must be brought to a complete stop to change rotation, and likewise if the propeller is *not* to rotate, the engine must be stopped. These operations require that an engineer be at the controls.

Propellers convert a rotating force into a linear force—thrust— by the *lift* created as their blades angle through the water. The hydrodynamics of this process dictate an optimum speed for those blades to do their best work. The propeller of a typical sailing vessel might work best at 500 to 700 revolutions per minute (RPM), but her diesel engine is likely to produce its best horsepower and efficiency at RPM on the order of 1500. The reduction gear, as its name indicates, reduces the ideal engine speed to the ideal propeller speed through a gear train. It is often included as part of the reverse gear unit and it is common to find a reverse/reduction gear unit attached directly to the crankshaft at the after end of an engine with the propeller shaft connected to that.

The end result of all of this is a thrust force produced by the propeller at the stern of the boat, and this is what we have to work with in handling the boat under power. What is the nature of this force, and what control do we have over it?

We can start it and stop it, either by starting and stopping the engine or engaging and disengaging the clutch if one is fitted.

We can direct it for *ahead* or *astern* propulsion depending on which way we run the engine or set the reverse gear. For ahead propulsion, the propeller thrust results in a forward push on the boat. This propelling force is almost directly in line with the boat's centerline, and for practical purposes the boat's response is to accelerate straight forward. The effect of the thrust going astern is slightly different and we will investigate that in a moment.

Finally, we can vary the strength of the thrust by varying the speed of the engine.

In terms of boat movement we can now make her go forward or backward, fast or slow, start from a stop, and bring her to a stop by using thrust opposite to her motion. In other words we have gas pedal, clutch, and brakes.

Steering is done by the rudder—mostly. As it was with handling the boat under sail there are many other forces affecting the movement of the boat at any moment and at times the rudder is ineffective or overpowered. Remember that the rudder's effect is the result of a flow of water past it. Look at the relative positions of the rudder and the propeller in Figure 6-2. With the engine going ahead, the propeller's thrust will be directed straight at the rudder, and no matter how fast the hull is actually moving there will be a strong flow of water past the rudder. It will be very effective with the engine going ahead.

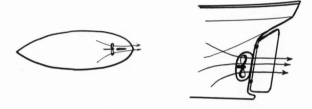

FIG. 6-2

With the engine going astern, however, the propeller's thrust is directed forward and there is no well-defined flow past the rudder until the whole boat has gathered considerable sternway. Therefore steering is poor when going astern. In addition, there is an effect known as the *walking effect,* which is likely to take over when the propeller is in reverse. This is caused by the uneven way that the propeller's thrust strikes the boat's hull when going astern. As shown in Figure 6-3, the water thrown forward by the propeller is also thrown somewhat sideways, imparting a sideways force to the hull on one side more than the other. Which way depends on the rotation of the propeller. Propellers are described as being either right- or left-handed. A right-hand propeller rotates to the right when pushing the boat forward, so it will be rotating to the left when going astern and will cause a walking effect which pushes the boat's stern to the left.

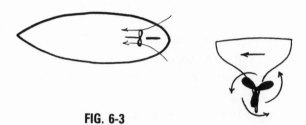

FIG. 6-3

The walking effect is usually quite pronounced and it is important that we be aware of which way and how much it will affect our vessel. We will take it into account when planning a maneuver so that it works for and not against us. Figure 6-4 shows the boat being turned in a confined space, a common maneuver. Assuming there are no other circumstances such as wind or current to be considered, we would plan this maneuver to take advantage of the propeller's walking effect. We know that we have a right-hand propeller so our boat will back to the left. Therefore, we will plan to turn the boat around to the right.

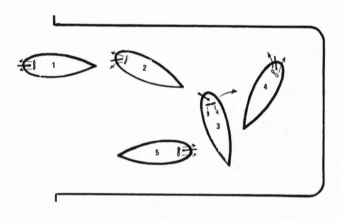

FIG. 6-4

In Position 2, we begin the turn by putting the helm to the right with the engine going ahead. The prop-wash on the rudder and the boat's headway make her begin to turn. In Position 3, we must go astern to stop our forward motion. When we do this the walking

FIG. 6-5

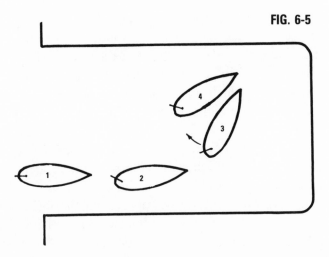

effect keeps the stern swinging to the left. The boat stops, then begins to gather sternway. Since the rudder is not very effective at slow speeds in reverse it can be left hard right during this time. In Position 4, we have run out of room behind us so we go ahead again with the engine. *As soon* as the propeller goes ahead it throws water against the rudder so that even before the boat stops moving backwards, the rudder's effect is as though she were going forward and is turning her more to the right. Depending on just how much space there is she may need to "back and fill" once or twice more to complete a 180° turn.

If we had attempted to turn the boat to the left the situation would have been as shown in Figure 6-5. In Position 3, as we started to back down to stop our headway, the walking effect would counteract our turn to the left and we would end up close to where we started, unable to turn her around.

Arriving at and departing from a dock are the other maneuvers that a boat must regularly perform at least once each voyage. These are delicate moments because at these times the boat, which may weigh a couple of hundred tons, is moving in very close proximity to terra-very-firma! Docks are almost by definition immovable objects, so if a dock and the boat were to come together at anything but the slowest of speeds serious damage would be done.

Every docking situation is unique and must be studied in advance as much as circumstances permit so that a plan can be made taking into account the boat, the space, the wind, the current, and any other special conditions that will affect the maneuver. No matter how carefully it is studied in advance, however, every situation contains surprises which inevitably appear at the most awkward moments, so whatever plan is made should include as many options and fallbacks as possible. These are times for very conservative thinking! What follows here are textbook examples. They almost never happen in real life, but they illustrate the fundamentals of getting the boat "on" and "off" the dock.

In Figure 6-6, Position 1, we are approaching the dock, intending to tie up the boat. We know that our boat has a right-hand propeller and walks to the left going astern, and for that reason we have chosen to land with our *port* side to the dock. If it is not clear why, it will be in a moment. Assuming no wind or current is affecting us, we steer to approach the dock as shown, at an angle of about 30° to 45°. We are moving dead slow, with just enough headway so that we can steer. At Position 2, it is time to go astern to stop the boat. We do this and as she stops, the walking effect moves the stern to the left as we anticipated. If we have timed everything just right, she will stop dead in the water right where we want to tie up, but *without contacting the dock* (Position 3). Now all that remains to be done is to get her against the dock and make the lines fast.

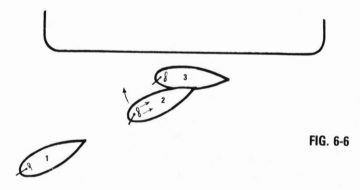

FIG. 6-6

The key to this final bit of maneuvering is the *dock lines*. Ultimately the boat will be secured to the dock with four dock lines, and these lines play an important role in bringing her safely alongside. Figure 6-7 shows how the four lines are arranged. They are often referred to by numbers from the bow to the stern for clarity. When the boat is secured at the dock, the *bow line* (#1) holds the bow in, the *stern line* (#4) holds the stern in, and #2 and #3, called *spring lines,* keep the boat from shifting forward or backward along the dock. These spring lines are most helpful in maneuvering.

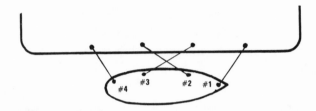

FIG. 6-7

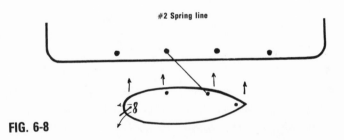

FIG. 6-8

Figure 6-8 shows the boat stopped five to ten yards away from the dock. The dock lines have been laid out on deck, ready for use. If they are heavy lines we will have also made ready a *heaving line* for each one. A heaving line is a light line about 100 feet long with a weighted end which can be thrown. Its other end is tied to the end of the dock line which is to be secured to the dock. As soon as the boat gets close enough, the heaving line for the #2 spring line is thrown ashore. A line handler on the dock will haul the dock line across and secure it to the dock in a position as shown. The slack is taken out of the line by the crew and it is made fast temporarily on the boat. Now the helm is put *hard right* and the propeller turned *slow ahead.* The thrust of the propeller does two things: it tries to drive the boat forward, and it hits the rudder and pushes the stern to the left.

In trying to move forward, the boat is restrained by the spring line, the effect of which is to pull her bow in toward the dock. This is matched by the prop-wash on the rudder pushing the stern toward the dock and the whole boat moves slowly sideways until she is resting against fenders. The combined effect of the engine, rudder, and spring line will hold her there until the other three lines are made fast, and then she is secure.

Leaving a berth alongside a dock is a bit different from pulling away from the curb in a car. A car steers with its front wheels, so turning them away from the curb and going forward is all that is needed (Figure 6-9).

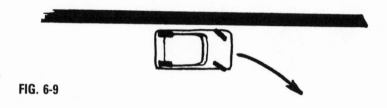

FIG. 6-9

A boat, however, is steered by her rudder at the stern, and the same strategy would not work. If we let go all the lines, put the rudder *hard right* and the propeller *ahead*, the stern would be slammed against the dock and the boat could not turn right. To get away we must first get her bow pointed out, then we can go forward. Once again a spring line is used.

In Figure 6-10, Frame 1, we have let go all the dock lines except the #3 spring line. The engine is started and propeller turned *slow astern*. The boat tries to move backwards but this is prevented by the spring. Instead the stern is pulled toward the dock and the bow rolled outward. Fenders must be placed carefully where the stern contacts the dock, but since the hull is not moving forward or back there is little likelihood of damage from the contact. Now that the bow is pointed out (Frame 2) we can simply go *slow ahead*, let go the #3 line and be off. In doing this it is good practice to put the rudder *hard left* toward the dock for a brief moment at first. This directs the prop-wash at the dock and pushes the stern clear. As

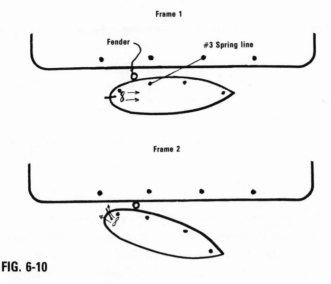

FIG. 6-10

soon as it is clear, the rudder should be put *amidships* or as needed for steering the boat on her way.

These examples illustrate some basic principles of handling an auxiliary sailing vessel under power. In practice, the situation is always more complicated and no matter how many examples are given none will match a real situation perfectly. Good shiphandling is a skill that is acquired by observation and practice. Knowledge of the handling characteristics of the particular boat is part of it, the rest is judgment gained from experience.

CHAPTER SEVEN

Electricity

Besides propulsion, the primary use of the diesel engine at sea is for generating electricity. The energy which arrived on board in the form of diesel fuel is converted once more into an extremely versatile form and put to use throughout the boat making light, heat, and cold; running motors for many purposes; and powering a great array of electronic devices. This chapter will look at how electricity is made, stored and used at sea.

The question of exactly what electricity *is,* and the details of how it does what it does, is not within the scope of this chapter, because our concern is only to know enough about it to be able to operate shipboard electrical equipment in a sensible manner. Electricity and electronics are sophisticated technologies, and unless the boat has budget and space enough to carry a technician, she will have to wait till she is in port for complex electrical repairs. The alternative is to carry duplicate or backup systems. Boats commonly have two (or more) generator sets, radios, radars, etc., for this reason.

Much of what we need to understand about electricity can be well explained by an analogy to water. Electricity is a form of potential energy like a supply of water in a standpipe or water tower. It takes energy to pump the water up into the tank, but once there, that energy can be reclaimed at any time by letting the water run back out. When electricity flows we call it a *current,* just as flowing water is a current. They both have energy and the ability to do work.

With electricity what flows is *electrons.* These particles, like most things, try to move from regions of high concentration or pressure to regions of less. Like the water in the tower which, if given a pipe to flow through will run to the ground, an accumulation of electrons will take any available path to reach a place with less electrons. Paths that electrons travel are called *conductors,* and some materials make better conductors than others. Most metals and water make notably good conductors, while glass, rubber, and most plastics are very poor. Materials that do not conduct are called *insulators.* Insulated copper wire is by far the most commonly used means of conducting electricity from one place to another. It is used throughout the boat, and it is very important that both the conductor inside and the insulator around it are intact and in good condition or, like a broken or leaky pipe, it will not carry the current to its destination.

There are three main reasons why electricity is such a useful form of energy: (1) It is easy to conduct relatively large amounts of it through wires from where it is produced to where it is used; (2) it can be converted into a wide variety of other useful forms of energy, or stored for later use; and (3) producing it *from* other forms of energy is a simple process.

The diagram in Figure 7-1 shows how electricity is produced, distributed, and used on a typical modern sailing vessel. An important feature of this system is that a generator only needs to run for a few hours a day. Most of the electricity the generator produces when running is stored in batteries for use during the rest of the day. We will now look closely at two ways of producing electricity, and a means of storing it aboard a boat.

Since an electric current is a flow of electrons, then to "make electricity" is to get electrons to flow. To get *water* to flow we arrange for an amount of it to be higher than water somewhere else. This can be done either by raising the water up to a higher place, or by making a lower place nearby (digging a hole). Either way we have created a *potential difference* between the two places, and water's response to a potential difference is to flow from high to low if a way can be found.

In just the same way, if we can create a potential difference between two places in terms of the number of electrons present, we

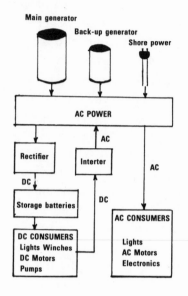

FIG. 7-1

can expect an electric current to flow from high to low when a conductor is offered. Lightning is a vivid example of huge numbers of electrons leaping from a place of high potential to one of low. In that case, the potential difference between the cloud and the ground is so great that the electrons jump through a relatively poor conductor: air.

Just as water can be raised more or less high, we can have potential differences of any size. Electrical potential difference is analogous to pressure and it is measured in *volts*. A greater potential difference (higher voltage) will drive the flow harder, and if the conductor is good enough, more current will flow. The actual quantity of electrons flowing, i.e., the volume of the current, is measured in *amps*. It should be apparent that the amount of current that is flowing in a given situation is a function of (a) the size of the potential difference driving it, and (b) the quality of the conductor through which it is traveling. This relationship is known as Ohm's law, which can be stated thus:

$$\text{Amps} = \text{Volts} \div \text{Ohms}$$

where ohms are a measure of the *resistance* that the conductor offers to the flow of electrons. The water analogy serves well to illustrate this fundamental relationship: the amount of water that flows through a hose is directly proportional to the pressure pushing it, and inversely proportional to the resistance of the hose.

Electricity is a transient form of energy. It takes energy to create a potential difference—work must be done—but this same amount of work will be returned to us (at least theoretically) when the electricity is converted into something else. When electricity lights a light, the energy of the flowing current is being converted into heat and light energy. The amount of work that the current is doing is a function of both the volume of the flow (amps) and the pressure driving it (volts) through the bulb. This is measured in *watts*, a unit of power. If it is a 100-watt bulb it requires 1 amp at 100 volts to light. Or it would light as well with 2 amps at 50 volts, ½ amp at 200 volts, etc. In electrical terms:

$$\text{Watts} = \text{Amps} \times \text{Volts}$$

These two formulas and the relationships they express are key to a general understanding of how electricity behaves. Take the time necessary to get an intuitive feel, using the water analogy if it helps, for what they mean.

There are many ways of creating a potential difference—an imbalance of electrons between two places—but only two are of concern to us on a boat. The first of these is by means of a chemical reaction, and the second is by magnetism.

MAKING ELECTRICITY CHEMICALLY

Take a grapefruit and stick a nail and a piece of copper wire into it. If you have a voltmeter with which to measure potential difference, you will find that one exists between the two metals. If we connect them together with a piece of wire, an electric current will flow through the wire from one to the other (Figure 7-2). Here is energy

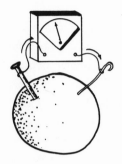

FIG. 7-2

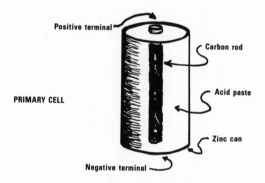

Positive terminal

Carbon rod

Acid paste

PRIMARY CELL

Zinc can

Negative terminal

FIG. 7-3

capable of doing (in this case a very small amount of) work. Where does the energy come from?

It comes from a chemical reaction that takes place between the two dissimilar metals and the acid of the grapefruit. How the reaction works we will leave for the chemists to discuss; it is sufficient for us to know that its result is an abundance of electrons on one of the metals and a scarcity of them on the other, which is what we are calling a potential difference. When we connect them we complete a *circuit* through which electrons will flow as long as the reaction in the grapefruit goes on robbing electrons from one metal and piling them up on the other. Eventually one of the metals will be consumed by the reaction and it will stop.

The grapefruit is an example of what is called a *primary cell*—a more familiar example of which is a flashlight battery. The term battery here is a misnomer, however, because it implies *many* cells whereas the item pictured in Figure 7-3 is a single cell. The primary cell shown is a true producer of electricity. Instead of two metals it uses zinc and carbon in an acid paste. One of these cells makes a potential difference of 1.5 volts. This is not very much voltage and cannot push much current. When more voltage is needed, however, it is a simple matter to combine cells together. When cells are combined we have a *battery*.

Cells can be combined either in *series* or in *parallel*. When they are combined in series (Figure 7-4), their potential differences add together so that the voltage of a four-cell battery will be six volts. The analogy here is to think of each cell as a water pump which raises water a certain amount. Connected in series, each pump lifts the water that amount to a higher tank, and at the end we have pressure from the highest tank.

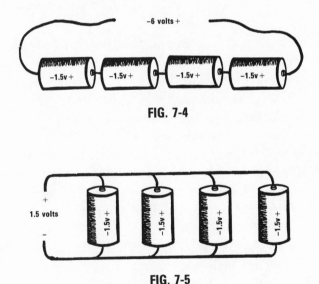

FIG. 7-4

FIG. 7-5

Connecting the cells in parallel (Figure 7-5) multiplies not the voltage but the amperage—volume of flow—available. It is as though each pump is raising its water to the same height, but the tanks are interconnected so the available volume of water is increased.

Notice that both series and parallel arrangements produce the same amount of power, it is only the ratio of amps to volts that is different. It is most common to find cells in series (e.g., in a flashlight) because most devices that use electricity work more efficiently at higher voltage and lower amperage. It is the *flow* which suffers from friction as it travels through conductors, so if we can do the same work with less flow at higher pressure we will lose less to friction.

As a means of producing electricity on the boat, primary cells are relatively minor. Flashlights, watches, and self-contained emergency devices such as radios depend on them, but they are heavy and bulky for the amount of power they produce, and they must be replaced when used up.

MAKING ELECTRICITY BY ELECTROMAGNETIC INDUCTION

The way most electrical power is made on boats and elsewhere is by a process called *electromagnetic induction*. As can be implied from its name, this is a process in which electrons are *induced* to flow, and it involves a close relationship between electricity and magnetism. This relationship is based upon the fact that electrons, as particles, have magnetic properties, and they are subject to the laws that govern how magnets react to other magnets, in particular the law that states that *like poles repel, and unlike poles attract each other.* Therefore an electron in the presence of a magnet will find itself either attracted or repelled, depending on the orientation of the magnet.

This suggests that perhaps a magnet could be employed to move some electrons, in which case we would have an electric current. This is precisely what is done in the device called an *alternator*. To see how the alternator works, let us first experiment with a magnet and a piece of wire conductor (Figure 7-6).

Wind a piece of wire into a coil and connect the two ends to a sensitive voltmeter to determine if any potential difference exists

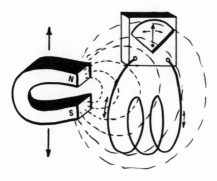

FIG. 7-6

between them. None does, for although the wire is naturally full of electrons, they are evenly distributed throughout it. Now, leaving the voltmeter connected, bring a magnet close to the coil and away again. The meter will move indicating potential difference between the ends of the wire. More than that, it will show that the difference was first one way and then the other as the magnet approached and moved away. Finally, put the magnet down on top of or right next to the coil. After initially showing a potential difference, the meter will return to zero for as long as the magnet and the coil do not move.

The magnet's force extends outward around it and we picture it as a *field* made up of *lines of force*. When the lines of force of the magnet approach the coil of wire and move through it, the electrons in the wire are sent piling to one end of the coil. When the magnet moves the other way the electrons are sent in the other direction. But if the magnet holds still relative to the coil, no electrons move.

We want to make electricity (create a flow of electrons) and to do that we must make a potential difference. If we arrange to move a coil of wire and a magnet relative to one another we will produce a potential difference. The only problems are that it is momentary, and changes direction. That it changes direction is inevitable; there is no way to move the two parts so that they are always approaching or always separating. But we can make the process continuous by mounting one or the other part on a shaft and rotating it next to or inside the other.

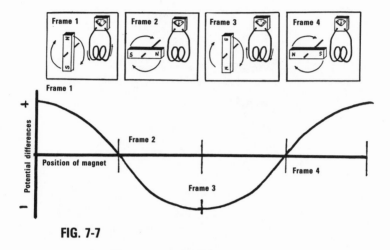

FIG. 7-7

Figure 7-7 illustrates the result of rotating the magnet next to a coil of wire. It is a simple alternator. If we keep the voltmeter connected while it turns, the changing potential difference during one revolution will be as shown at the bottom. If instead of the voltmeter, we connected a light bulb to the ends of the coil, the changing potential difference would send a flow of electrons back and forth through the bulb. This would make the bulb glow intermittently, which, if fast enough, would fool the eye and seem continuous.

What we have found is that the alternator generates *alternating current,* a current that moves back and forth instead of constantly in one direction as did the *direct current* from the primary cell. This is not a problem. Both are quite capable of doing work, just as a water wheel would get the grain ground equally well whether it turned the millstone back and forth, or in one direction. Some electrical devices are particular about running only on AC or only on DC, but others, like light bulbs, do well on either. In fact, AC has many advantages over DC, some of which we will touch on, and it has become the standard type of current supplied to homes and industry throughout the world. One important advantage that we have already seen is that it is so simple to produce.

The alternator in Figure 7-7 needs a few refinements before it will be an effective producer of electric power. The typical alternator found on a boat has the magnet mounted on a shaft and turning inside the coils of wire. To increase its efficiency there are many coils, the magnet has several pairs of poles instead of one, and it is rotated very fast. The mechanical force to rotate it, which is the energy being converted to electrical form, is supplied by the crank-shaft of a diesel engine.

STORAGE OF ELECTRICITY:
THE SECONDARY CELL

As mentioned previously, one of the requirements we have of the electrical system aboard our boat is that the electricity produced at one time can be stored for future use. Electricity is stored in *secondary cells*, which are grouped together and called batteries. Unlike a primary cell, the secondary cell does not *produce* electricity, it will only *store* electricity that has been produced somewhere else. The battery in a car is a battery of secondary cells. When it is new it has no "charge," that is, there is no potential difference between its terminals. It must be charged by connecting it to a source of electric power.

A secondary cell is made of two lead plates in an acid solution. Because the two plates are the same metal, there is initially no potential difference between them. When they are connected to an external potential difference, however, a chemical reaction takes place which causes electrons to be moved from one plate to the other. When the charging process is completed and the external "charge" disconnected, the electron imbalance remains between the plates, so that a potential difference now exists between them. If a circuit is provided from plate to plate a current will flow, and can do work until the potential of the plates becomes even again. Then we say the battery is dead, and needs to be recharged.

The storage capacity of a single secondary cell is small, but they can be combined in the same ways that primary cells were combined to make batteries of various sizes. The familiar car battery is made up of six two-volt cells in series. When it is charged it has a potential difference of 12 volts, which is what automotive electrical systems use. A large ship is likely to use higher voltage for its electrical system. A standard size for large batteries is eight volts (four two-volt cells in series), and it is common to connect these in series to supply electrical systems of 24, 32, or 120 volts.

THE RECTIFIER

To charge secondary cells we must cause a chemical reaction which will push electrons one way in the cell. This is done by connecting the cell to an outside potential difference, but it must be a constant one—always in the same direction. In other words, we must have a source of *direct current* to charge a storage battery. The current we are generating with our alternator is *alternating current* and if we connected that to a secondary cell there would be no net transfer of electrons in one direction. Apparently if we are to be able to store the electricity we produce with the alternator we must first convert it from AC to DC. This is accomplished by a device called a *rectifier*.

The key element in the rectifier is the *diode,* which is to an electric current what a *check valve* is to a flow of water. A check valve (Figure 7-8) allows flow to happen in one direction but prevents it from reversing. The diode has the same property. Inserted into an electric circuit, it permits electrons to flow through it in one direction only. In a DC circuit as shown, this would mean either the light would be lit or not, depending which way the diode was oriented relative to the current.

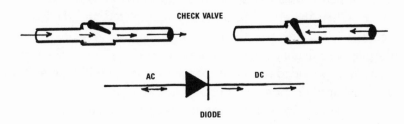

FIG. 7-8

In an AC circuit, however, current is alternating back and forth, and electrons are surging first one way then the other. A diode placed in this circuit will pass every "surge" in one direction and block all the others. The result will be pulses of current moving through the circuit in the same direction—an intermittent DC. But since half of the AC has been blocked we have lost half our power.

The solution to this problem is an arrangement of four diodes known as a *bridge rectifier*. Figure 7-9 diagrams how the four diodes are connected. The top and bottom corners of the diagram are connected to the AC circuit. Remembering that the current in an AC circuit moves back and forth, trace the paths the electrons must follow to get from top to bottom, and from bottom to top, alternately. It can only pass through a diode in the direction of its arrow. It will be seen that what results is a continuous flow of current in one direction through the DC circuit, which is connected to the right and left corners.

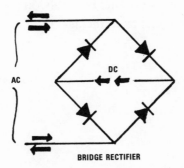

BRIDGE RECTIFIER

FIG. 7-9

Now we are able to produce AC electric power by using a diesel engine to turn an alternator, convert some or all of that power into DC in a bridge rectifier and use the DC to charge storage batteries. Once they are charged we can shut off the diesel and supply the electrical needs of the boat from the batteries. Of course the batteries only give us DC, so if we have any devices aboard that will only operate on AC we have another problem. Either we can only use them when the alternator is running, or we must have another means of *re*converting some of the batteries' DC into AC. There is such a means called an *inverter,* an electronic device which produces an alternating current from direct current.

One final word about efficiency before leaving this chapter. From the start, what we have really been looking at is *energy conversion* as it applies to our modern sailing vessel. From mechanical advantages gained through simple machines, to generating forces in fluid flows, to converting stored solar energy in diesel fuel into everything from propulsion to electric power for subsequent conversion into hundreds of forms, all our devices have been energy converters of one sort or another. Theoretically, when energy undergoes a conversion none is lost or gained, and we have generally maintained a theoretically ideal view as we investigated these energy converters. Of course the reality is that every time we convert energy some of it is lost to us, as friction, waste heat, slippage, etc., and always will be. By the time we plug in our AC-powered device, we have lost energy in the inverter, in the battery, in the rectifier, in the alternator, in the diesel engine—and probably on top of all this the bosun has snitched some fuel from the daytank to clean his paintbrushes!

CHAPTER EIGHT

Introduction to Navigation

Navigation is the process of finding out and keeping track of the boat's whereabouts, and directing her toward her destination. The techniques and procedures involved are fundamentally no different than those we employ unconsciously as we move around in our environment. Walking around the house, down the street, driving a car, and planning a trip all require navigational skills which we instinctively possess, our mind having developed the ability to process primarily visual inputs and turn them into deductions about our location, our course, and our speed relative to the things around us.

We know where we are—and, if asked, would describe our position—by referring to those things in our surroundings we recognize. "I'll meet you across the street from the A & P," defines a position by relating it to a known *reference point*. As we walk across a room we automatically calculate our progress as we pass pieces of furniture and triangulate the distance to the exit door. If at a given moment we had to describe our position precisely we might say we were at the edge of the rug by the piano bench, using those items as our known reference points.

Notice that for a reference point to be of any value it must satisfy two requirements: (1) it must be *identifiable* so that we, and anyone else involved, will not mistake it for some other point; and (2) its *location* must be known to all parties concerned. Then, and only then, can we make some kind of *measurement* that will relate us to the reference point and begin to define our position.

All navigation depends on reference points of one kind or another, so we will always need to be aware of *what* it is (identify), *where* it is (locate), and then how it relates to us (measure). We must also be aware that the resulting knowledge of our whereabouts will only be as accurate as the accuracy with which we identified, located, and measured the reference point. If we mistake the Stop and Shop for the A & P, or we do not remember that the piano bench has been moved over by the fireplace, or if we are really closer to the middle of the rug than the edge, then our resulting positions are going to be in error.

We can divide navigation into five categories, each one defined by the kind of reference points it uses. The first we will call *eyeball navigation,* and it is simply the process of locating and directing the boat, usually in close quarters, by watching the surroundings. A tour around a crowded harbor in a rowboat would be an exercise in eyeball navigation. The reference points are familiar, their positions known and the measurements can be done by eye because the distances are small.

As we move farther away from the reference points, it eventually becomes impossible to make accurate judgements of distance by eye, so we go to the graphic techniques of *piloting* for the triangulation that our eyes were able to do before. Our reference points are still visible (or audible in some cases), but for identifying and locating them we must learn to read and use nautical charts and reference publications.

Electronic navigation uses piloting techniques, but its reference points are sources of radio signals of various kinds. These must be identified and measured by electronic devices, and are effective when distance or lack of visibility have obscured other reference points.

When neither visible nor electronic reference points are available, as is the case far offshore, there are still some very dependable ones available for *celestial navigation.* Whenever the horizon can be seen simultaneously with either the sun, moon, planets, or stars, these heavenly bodies can serve as reference points to the navigator. The process of celestial navigation is the same as for the others: identify, locate and measure.

Finally, there is the kind of navigation known as *dead reckoning* (the name derives from *ded*uced reckoning), which is carried on whenever the boat is moving and none of the reference points mentioned so far are available. Dead reckoning also uses piloting techniques, but its reference point is the last *known* position of the boat. In the absence of other more solid information, the present position of the boat is "reckoned" from the last known position by accounting for direction and distance travelled in the interim. Positions derived by dead reckoning are subject to many inaccuracies, but frequently they are all that is available and are therefore a very important part of the picture.

When a boat is underway, navigation is a continuous process which ends only when she arrives at her destination. Whether it is the job of one person designated as navigator, or shared by several people on a rotating basis, it is always a major concern in the operation of the boat. The actual amount of time and attention that is spent on navigation is entirely a function of the boat's current circumstances, and how urgently and precisely her position must be known. Well offshore on a long passage, it may be quite sufficient to fix her position once a day by a few celestial observations, each requiring about 15 minutes to work out. But there are many reasons why it may be important to have hourly, half-hourly, or even minute-by-minute knowledge of the boat's position, and then the navigator becomes very busy, for although boats do not move very fast, neither can they change their course and speed very quickly. At both ends of the offshore passage the boat must be operated in close quarters where accurate navigation is critical to safety. The navigator must use his judgment to determine how much attention the situation requires.

To be a good navigator, one must recognize that the job is never done. Until the voyage is over, the boat's position is always in question, and therefore the strategy for getting to the destination is constantly in need of revision. A good navigator is always thinking several steps ahead of the present, anticipating what may happen to the extent that his experience enables him. Whether it is the next bend in the channel a hundred yards ahead, or the landfall three days away, he wants to be prepared, and thereby better able to cope with the unexpected—which it is usually best to expect! He should develop a "what if" attitude, pose himself as many variations on an upcoming situation as he can, and have contingency plans thought out and ready. "What if it is foggy when we are making our landfall? Are there foghorns or sound buoys we can use for references? What if there is a very large tanker coming around the next bend of the channel? Is there enough water to get out of the way?"

A good navigator will make use of all available input to confirm his hypothesis about the boat's position. Two observations may theoretically be all that is necessary to establish a position, but if a third, fourth, and fifth are available it is negligent not to use them to verify the first two. Every new reference point that appears should be checked to see if it agrees with the others, because if it does not, there has been a mistake made somewhere and it is just possible that it means that the boat is not where the navigator thinks it is.

Finally, a good navigator works neatly. There is very little about navigation that is complicated, but nearly everything is subject to careless errors. About the only way to combat careless errors is to make a habit of working methodically and neatly. Entries in log books, plotting work on charts, and sight reductions worked out in notebooks should all be clearly decipherable to others, because, at a later time, it may be necessary to check back to locate an error or reconstruct a situation. The safety of the boat depends on good communication among those in control, and navigators communicate through what they have written down. It must be clear!

Eyeball navigation is self-explanatory, and electronic navigation only differs from piloting in that electronic devices do the measuring. The chapters that follow will outline the fundamentals of dead reckoning, piloting, and celestial navigation.

CHAPTER NINE

Location:
Distance and Direction

There are many ways to describe the location of something, but to be perfectly accurate we have to employ some kind of *coordinate system* to positively define its position. "My hat is on my seat" locates my hat for anyone who knows which is my seat, but for anyone else to find my hat I would have to say, "My hat is on the third seat in the tenth row" to effectively describe its position. Rows and seat numbers are a type of coordinate system.

Positions on the earth are defined by such a coordinate system, and before we can describe the location of our boat we must be familiar with this system. The earth is a sphere spinning around an axis of rotation which intersects the earth's surface at two points. These two fixed points, the *north pole* and *south pole,* are the basis for the coordinate system we use. Figure 9-1 shows the earth as seen from two different points of view. These two views are necessary in order to picture a three-dimensional sphere on a flat piece of paper and we will use them throughout this discussion of navigation. In the first case, we are seeing a side view of the sphere. Both poles are visible and the center of the earth can also be shown. In addition, we can show the *equator* by a straight line through the center, equidistant from the poles. In the second diagram, we are looking up at the earth from below the south pole. That pole and the center coincide, and the equator is seen as the earth's circumference.

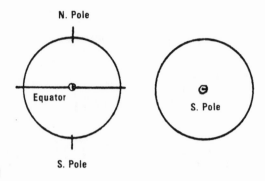

N. Pole

Equator

S. Pole

S. Pole

FIG. 9-1

With reference to the poles, we can now begin to describe the position of a point on the surface of the sphere. The point could be *at* the north or south pole, but if it is not (which in the case of our boat is more likely) then it is some *distance* from them. The farthest it could be from both poles would be on the equator, and the equator has come to be used as the starting point *from* which to measure distance *toward* one pole or the other.

When we say "distance" we normally think of units of miles or feet or some sort of length, but if we picture our boat on the side view of the earth we can see that her distance from the equator could also be expressed as an angle, which has its vertex at the center of the earth (Figure 9-2). The relationship between an angle with its vertex at the earth's center and distance on the earth's surface is of great importance to navigators. The *nautical mile* has been established as the unit of distance for navigation and by definition one nautical mile is the equivalent of one minute (1/60th of a degree) of arc formed at the earth's surface by such an angle. (It happens to be slightly longer than the statute mile in use ashore (6,076 feet instead of 5,280). Thus we can either say the boat is 30°, or 1,800 nautical miles (30 × 60) from the equator. If we choose to express the distance from the equator as an angle in degrees then we have stated the boat's *latitude*.

Latitude is one coordinate of the earth's coordinate system. By saying the boat's latitude is 30° we have begun to locate the boat on the surface of the earth. We now know that she is 30° (or 1,800 miles) from the equator. But on which side of it? There is an obvious ambiguity until we specify whether the boat is 30° *north* or 30° *south* of the equator, and as soon as we do that we have the concept of *direction*. Direction is always relative to something, and in this case we again refer to the poles. In Figure 9-2 the boat is 30° *north* of the equator, that is, *toward* the north pole. Properly stated, her latitude is 30° North.

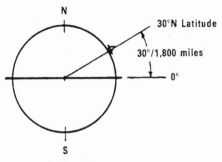

FIG. 9-2

This tells us something about the boat's location, but not enough. "My hat is on a seat in the tenth row" is helpful but not precise. With the information we now have, our boat could be anywhere on a line running around the earth 30° north of the equator. We need another means to enable us to say where on that circle she is located. A circle, being what it is, has no beginning or end which we can use as a reference to locate a point on it—unless we arbitrarily establish one. As soon as we do that we can say that the point in question is so far to one side or the other of the designated point (Figure 9-3).

FIG. 9-3

For the second coordinate on earth, an arbitrary reference point has been established at Greenwich, England, which is used as the starting point for measuring *longitude*. The longitude of a point on the earth's surface is simply the angle formed at the center of the earth between the point and the closest spot on a line from pole to pole passing through Greenwich. In Figure 9-4, our boat is shown on the south pole view of the earth along with the line through Greenwich and the poles. The angle between them is the boat's longitude, in this case 75°.

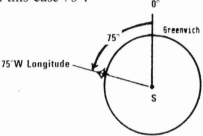

FIG. 9-4

As with latitude there is an ambiguity since longitude is measured to the *closest* point on the line through Greenwich. The boat could be 75° on one side or the other, so we must specify. Again we refer to the poles for direction and this time call longitude that is to the left of the direction to the north pole *west,* and that to the right, *east.* So the boat's longitude as pictured is correctly described as 75° West.

Current practice is to express latitude and longitude in degrees, minutes, and tenths of a minute. In stating a position it is usual to give the latitude first. Thus the position of a boat might be written in the log book as: Lat. 44 12.7 N × Long. 62 53.1 W. Notice that it is not necessary to use symbols for degrees and minutes, but that a space is left between the digits. The designators N and W must be included.

We now have a means of positively and precisely defining positions on the earth. In developing this coordinate system of latitude and longitude we have also gained a unit of distance, the nautical mile, and the basis for describing direction based on the direction to the north pole.

Nautical miles are normally figured to the nearest tenth, and they are referred to simply as *miles,* since only nautical miles are used in navigation. It is worthwhile to think about the relationship between miles and angle, or arc, again, and to notice a couple of useful facts. Make side- and bottom-view drawings to help visualize that if we drew lines parallel to the equator to represent every degree of latitude they would all be 60 miles apart. However, if we drew a line for every degree of longitude, they would be 60 miles apart only at the equator, and would get closer together as they approached the poles. The practical significance of this becomes evident when we measure distances on a chart or plotting sheet, which has latitude and longitude scales printed on its edges. No matter where in the world we are, it is correct to use the latitude scale as a mile scale: a minute of *latitude* will always be a nautical mile. But unless we happen to be on the equator, the same is not true for a minute of longitude. Be sure *not* to use the longitude scale as a mile scale!

FIG. 9-5

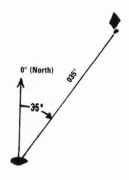

FIG. 9-6

Direction on the surface of the earth is nowadays expressed almost exclusively in degrees, measured clockwise from the direction to the north pole or *true north*, through 360°. The use of *points* (see Figure 9-5) is only found in describing weather phenomena such as wind direction or sea direction. For most navigational purposes, accuracy to the whole degree is adequate, and directions are always spoken and written in three digits, for example the true direction from the boat to the buoy in Figure 9-6 is 035, written without need of the degree symbol, and spoken aloud as "zero, three, five," for maximum clarity.

The latitude and longitude coordinate system enables us to define locations, and we have the means to quantify and express distance and direction. Now we can push off from the shore and begin the process of keeping track.

CHAPTER TEN

Keeping Track

As we pull away from the dock and maneuver through the harbor we depend on our eyes to locate us and keep track of our progress among reference points which are close at hand. We need only *relative* direction—relative to the dock or channel—and distances which we judge by eye because they are small. Before long, however, we have moved far enough away so that we cannot be accurate just by eye. The reference points we see are now in the distance, and the exact direction and distance of our progress is not clear by simply watching the shore. We must call on some tools and techniques for accuracy.

THE BASIC TOOLS

Two basic tools are required in order to keep track of a boat's progress. The *compass* and the *log*, both ancient tools and found in various forms on ships for centuries, are still as important as ever even in this age of electronics.

The magnetic compass indicates the direction the boat is being steered relative to the earth's *magnetic* north pole. For many reasons, the boat may not actually be traveling in that direction, but it is a starting point for the navigator in determining the direction of the boat's progress. In using the compass we must be aware that it rarely shows us *true* direction, that is, direction based on the earth's north pole as its reference. It is subject to error from the fact that the earth's geographic north pole and its magnetic north pole are not in the same place (called *variation*), and is also subject to local error caused by magnetic disturbances on the boat itself (called *deviation*). To a large extent these errors can be known and compensated for, and thus are not so much an obstacle for the navigator, but rather a bit of routine which must be learned and remembered whenever the compass is used.

Variation—the amount of discrepancy between magnetic and true north—is different in different parts of the world, and even changes slowly over time (years). But it is predictable and known, so that with a source of this information at hand, the navigator can tell how much variation is affecting his compass and correct for it. Present variation, and the rate of change of variation is shown on most local charts, and on special charts of the world as well.

Deviation is unique to the particular compass on the particular boat, and is found by an exercise known as "swinging ship." In most cases the deviation error can be eliminated by placing small compensating magnets near the compass to counteract the local disturbances. If this is successfully done, the compass then points accurately at the magnetic north pole.

Even when the compass errors are known and accounted for we cannot assume for certain that the boat is moving over the earth in the direction the compass shows. A sailing vessel always makes leeway, or slips sideways, somewhat; ocean or tidal currents may carry her in another direction; or poor helmsmanship may cause her to travel a sightly different course than intended. These are factors that the navigator may or may not be aware of. To the extent that he is, he can allow or compensate for them, and it is largely a matter of experience to know what to look for and how to respond.

In spite of a long list of reasons why it is not perfect, the compass is by far the most important navigational tool we have. Used wisely, it is reliable day and night, in all weather, and is the source of all our information about direction.

Distance traveled is measured by the log. This device actually measures how much water moves past the boat. It consists of a spinner or propeller either towed behind the boat at the end of a long line or protruding from the hull of the boat underwater. The spinner is attached to a clockwork system of gears or an electronic counter. As the spinner rotates it causes pointers on a dial or digits on a display screen to translate the number of rotations into nautical miles. The log reading is noted when the boat leaves her point of departure and read cumulatively until she once again resumes eyeball navigation on making port. Normally the log is read every hour and the number of miles traveled in that hour can be found by subtracting the previous hour's reading.

Like the compass, the log is subject to error. Since it measures the boat's progress *through the water* it may not be indicating the boat's true progress *over the bottom*. If the water itself is in motion due to a current of any kind this motion would have to be combined with the boat's motion through the water to find her true distance traveled. When current is known, this can be done. Another common cause for error in the log's reading is due to seaweed fouling the spinner. It is important to check it at regular intervals.

DEAD RECKONING

With these two tools the boat's progress is recorded. Presumably we departed from a known point. A navigator wants to know this *point of departure* as precisely as possible, so usually a clear reference point such as a buoy is chosen for this purpose as the boat heads out to sea. What begins at the point of departure is *dead reckoning*. Dead reckoning is the process of deducing your present location from knowledge of how far, and in what direction you have traveled from a known point. It is a form of navigation that is carried on all the time the boat is at sea. Dead reckoning information is recorded graphically on the chart or plotting sheet, and is also written in the boat's logbook. Although it is frequently less accurate than other kinds of navigation, it is often the only kind of information that is available on a regular basis about the boat's position, and therefore is extremely important.

It is usual practice at sea to show a dead reckoning (DR) position for the boat every hour on the hour. In Figure 10-1 we have left our point of departure—a buoy—at 0700. At 0800 we take information from the compass and log to find out where we are. After accounting for deviation, variation, and all other sources of error, we know from the compass that we have been moving in the direction 282. This single piece of information tells us a great deal—but not all—about where we are. Instead of the possibility of being anywhere at all on the chart, we can now eliminate all positions except those which lie in the direction 282 from our starting point. To show all these possibilities graphically we can draw a straight line from the buoy in the direction 282. If we are confident in the information from the compass, we must be on that line somewhere.

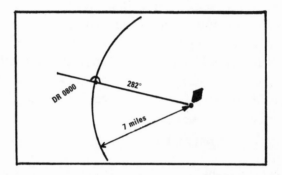

FIG. 10-1

Reading the log at 0800 we find that we have travelled seven miles through the water. This, too, tells us a lot, but not everything. If we assume that the log's reading is true and not affected by current or weeds, then we must be in a position which is seven miles away from the buoy. That fact can be graphically represented by drawing a circle of seven-mile radius with its center at the buoy. We must be on the circle.

Separately, each of these bits of information tell us something, but together they define a single point. When both the line representing our direction, and the circle representing our distance are drawn together we find only one point which is common to both. That is our position by dead reckoning at 0800. The point is marked by a dot with a half-circle and labelled "0800 DR." An hour later we can record our direction and distance traveled since 0800 and produce a new DR position for 0900, and so on for each hour as the boat proceeds we will have a "reckoning" of our location.

At this point we must stop and look very critically at these DR positions. Just how valid is a DR position? There is no general answer to that question. It depends on how we assess the accuracy of all the "inputs" that went into defining the position. There are many possible sources of error in each of those inputs, several of which have been described already, and in addition we must realize that since each hourly position is reckoned from the previous hour's position, there is the likelihood of errors accumulating from hour to hour. In general it must be clear that a DR position is very "iffy," and a prudent navigator will never depend solely on one. As has been mentioned before, the value of dead reckoning lies in the fact that there are times when there is no better information available, and at those times dead reckoning is the difference between *no* idea where we are and *some* idea where we are.

But how then can we be *sure* of our position? When do we get positive, reliable information that we can count on to tell us exactly where we are with our boat? The answer to that is: any time we can measure the distance or direction of an *identifiable reference point, whose position is known to us.*

THE LINE OF POSITION AND THE FIX

Suppose we left a known point of departure and carried on our DR for several hours, and now we need to have more certain knowledge of our whereabouts in order to safely approach the coast again. If landmarks and aids to navigation such as buoys and lighthouses are in sight, then we will be able to employ *piloting* techniques to determine our position. We look around us and select a reference point which we can identify, locate and measure. The lighthouse shown in Figure 10-2 is identified by day by its description, and by night by the characteristics of its light, in the *Light List*—the publication listing all aids to navigation. Our chart also indicates the light's characteristics, and, most importantly, it shows the precise location of the lighthouse.

The lighthouse is identified and located, so how do we measure? Probably the most common way to measure a visible reference point in piloting is to *take a bearing* on it. By sighting the lighthouse across our compass, we measure the direction that it lies *from* our

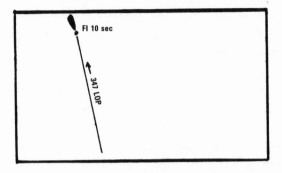

FIG. 10-2

boat: 347. As soon as we know that (and we must not neglect to take those compass errors into account) we know for certain that we have to be one of the *set of points* from which the lighthouse bears 347. That set of points can be shown on the chart by drawing a straight line from the lighthouse back in the direction opposite to 347. That line includes all the possible places from which the lighthouse would appear in that direction, and we call this line a *line of position (LOP)*.

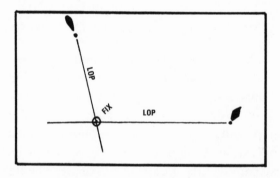

FIG. 10-3

LOPs can take many forms, but every one is the result of a measurement of a known reference point, and thus is a set of points, one of which is our position. The LOP in Figure 10-2 is a straight line which resulted from a bearing taken on the lighthouse. If instead we measured the distance to the lighthouse, by using radar or by vertical sextant angle, for example, and found that we were 9.3 miles from it, then we could draw a circular LOP around the lighthouse 9.3 miles in radius and know that we were one of the points on it. Or if we measured the depth of the water with a leadline or fathometer and found it to be 10 fathoms deep, we could draw a 10-fathom contour line on our chart following the soundings given there, and know that we were one of the points on *that* line.

A single line of position locates us within a certain set of points, but if we can obtain two different LOPs that are true for the same time we can eliminate all possibilities except points which belong to both sets. Graphically this means that we must be at the point (or one of the points) where the LOPs intersect (Figure 10-3). The intersection of two or more *simultaneous* LOPs is called a *fix* and the point is circled on the chart. To qualify as a fix, a position must be defined by *two or more LOPs which are true for the same time,* and therefore a fix is a position of which the navigator is certain. Dead reckoning information does not qualify and should never be accepted as part of a fix.

Two LOPs are theoretically all that are needed for a fix, but whenever there are more reference points available it is good practice to obtain one or more additional LOPs—bearings, distances-off, soundings, etc.—and use them to check the first two. Ideally, all LOPs taken at the same time should intersect at a single point: the boat's position. When several are plotted, however, any inaccuracy in any part of the process of identifying, locating, and measuring will show up as a less-than-perfect intersection. For example (Figure 10-4), it is not uncommon to find after plotting three bearings that the lines intersect forming a triangle instead of a single point. It is impossible to be perfectly accurate taking bearings, so a small triangle is inevitable, and the circumstances of the situation must determine whether the size of the triangle is acceptable or not. If it is, the center of the triangle is taken as the fix.

With both dead reckoning and piloting techniques in hand we are equipped to navigate our boat anywhere except for long periods of time offshore. For that we will need to be able to use the celestial reference points to obtain lines of position, but for a passage of a day or two we could get by on dead reckoning, until we again picked up landmarks or aids to navigation.

Once the boat is clear of the harbor, dead reckoning goes on continuously and fixes are obtained whenever possible as needed.

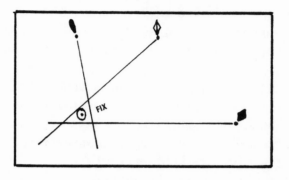

FIG. 10-4

Whenever a fix is plotted, the dead reckoning is restarted from the new known position. At this time, it is important to study the difference between the new fix and the DR position for the same time and to try to explain what has caused the difference. Much can be learned from this about leeway, currents, and the like, which we can subsequently take into account as the boat goes on.

ALLOWING FOR CURRENT

In Figure 10-5, we have departed from the buoy at 1400 and an hour later we plot our DR and get a fix from three bearings. The DR is where we thought we were based on direction and distance traveled according to the compass and the log. The fix is where we find we really are at 1500. We attribute the difference to *current.*

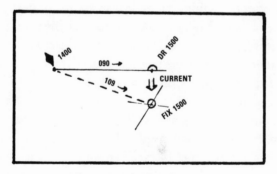

FIG. 10-5

A line from the point of departure to the DR position represents our motion *through the water* for the hour—direction and distance. A line from the point of departure to the fix shows our actual motion *over the bottom* during the same time. Although we steered 090 and went six miles through the water, we actually progressed in the direction 109 for a distance of 6.4 miles. The reason for this is that the water itself was moving also. Apparently during the hour from 1400 to 1500 the water moved south (180) two miles. There was no way for us to know this until we got a fix which we could compare with the DR. Of course as the water moved, we were carried along with it, and so its motion combined with our own causing us to end up at the fix.

The whole situation can be very neatly shown by using vectors to represent (1) the boat's motion through the water, (2) the water's motion, called current, and (3) the actual *track* of the boat over the bottom. Each vector has two dimensions: direction and length. The *ship vector* represents the direction the boat is steering by compass, and her speed through the water as measured by the log in an hour. The *current vector* shows the direction the current is *setting,* and its rate of *drift*—how far it flows in an hour. The *track vector* shows the direction the boat truly moves and her speed over the bottom.

As long as we make each of these three vectors represent the same time period—normally one hour—we can show that:

Ship vector + Current vector = Track vector

To add two vectors together graphically, they are placed head-to-tail. Their sum will be found by completing the triangle (Figure 10-6).

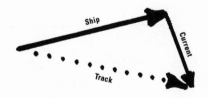

FIG. 10-6

Thus, going back to our situation at 1500, as we set off from our fix at 1500 we know that a current setting 180 at two knots (nautical miles per hour) will be adding its motion to our own, still 090 at six knots. We should be able to predict where we will end up at 1600 by adding together the current vector and the ship vector and finding the track.

It makes no difference in which order we add them, as long as we place them head-to-tail, so for the sake of consistency we plot current first when it is known. The current vector is drawn starting from the point where the boat is (the 1500 fix), in the direction 180, and two miles long—the distance it will move in one hour. Be sure to place an arrowhead on it to make clear which way it is going. The ship vector is to be added to it, so it is attached to its head and drawn in the direction that the boat is being steered (090) for a length corresponding to the boat's distance traveled through the water in an hour—six miles. The triangle is then completed giving us the direction and length of the track or actual motion of the boat for the hour. At 1600 we can expect to be at the position shown, having again traveled 6.4 miles in the direction 109.

A different but very common situation is that in which we know there is a current affecting the boat's progress, and we want to allow for it in planning a course to take us to a given point.

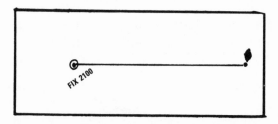

FIG. 10-7

In Figure 10-7, we want to go from the 2100 fix to the buoy, and we know that there is a current setting 315 at 1.5 knots. We also know that our boat will be making seven knots through the water. What course should we steer the boat? If we simply headed directly for the buoy, common sense tells us we will end up somewhere to the left of it, so we should be able to compensate for that by steering a bit to the right of the direct line, but how much?

We can answer that graphically with our same vectors, by building a model of what will happen in one hour. Of the three vectors what information do we have to work with? A good procedure is to make a table (Figure 10-8) with spaces for each of the two dimensions of the three vectors, and fill in what is known. In this case we know both dimensions of the current vector: we know the length of the ship vector (our speed through the water), and we know the direction of the track vector (the direction we want to actually travel). What is not known is the direction of the ship vector (course to steer) and the length of the track vector (how fast we will actually progress toward the buoy).

	Speed	Dir.
Ship	7	?
Current	1.5	315
Track	?	090

FIG. 10-8

As long as we know four of the six dimensions we can find the others by building a triangle. Again, current is known so we will start by drawing the current vector from the starting point, the 2100 fix. This time it points 315 and is 1.5 miles long. This shows how the water will move in an hour. The line from the fix to the destination buoy *contains* the track vector—we want our track to be in that direction, but as yet we do not know how fast we will progress along it so we cannot indicate its length with an arrowhead. (It is essential to keep in mind that the vectors show what happens in *one hour,* and the triangle we build may not reach all the way to our destination.) Of the third vector (the ship) we know its length but not its direction. We also know that its tail will attach to the current vector's head and then it will close a triangle by touching the track vector. Simply measure the seven-mile length with dividers or a strip of paper, connect one end to the current vector's head, and swing the other end until it meets the track.

As soon as the triangle is complete we have the missing information. The direction of the ship vector is the course to steer the boat to exactly compensate for the current, and the length of the track vector is the speed we will move over the bottom toward the buoy. The reality of what happens is shown in Figure 10-9. Our boat is located at the 2100 fix, and sets out for the buoy steering 100. This course plus the effect of the current cause her to travel slightly sideways along the track line, and a bit slower than her speed through the water. At the end of an hour she is at the corner of the triangle, but if the current does not change and she does not change her course or speed, she will continue to track along the line to the buoy, reaching it about 45 minutes later.

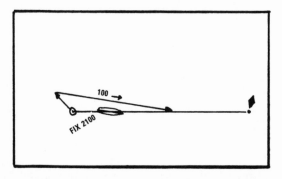

FIG. 10-9

Any current situation can be solved by building the vector triangle. First make a table of known dimensions, then build the triangle, remembering to start with current when it is one of the known quantities. The ship and current vectors must be placed head-to-tail, and the third side will be the track, the route the boat actually travels.

THE RUNNING FIX

It frequently happens both in piloting and in celestial navigation that only one reference point is available at a given time—for example a single lighthouse, or the sun. This means that we can only obtain a single LOP, not enough for a fix. A bearing on the lighthouse taken at 0930 tells us only that we are one of the points on the line of position shown in Figure 10-2. Although no other LOP is available at 0930, there is a technique whereby we can obtain a fix by taking a second bearing on the same lighthouse. This is called a *running fix*. While it is not as certain as a true fix, in the absence of anything better it can be very useful information.

A running fix is obtained by the process of "advancing a line of position." The key to understanding this process is remembering that an LOP is a set of possible positions for the boat. Our bearing on the lighthouse has told us that at 0930 we were among the set of points comprising a particular line. If someone demanded that we show him where we were at 0930, we would have to answer not by naming a point but by drawing a line—the only honest answer we could make based on the information we have. So for the time being we will let the line represent the position of our boat.

Now our boat is underway, not standing still. As time passes we are sailing northeast on a course of 045 by the compass and making five knots by the log, and we will assume that this is the actual course and speed we are traveling over the bottom. So, in an hour's time, we will have moved five miles in the direction of 045. If we knew where we were at 0930, and we know how far and in what direction we have travelled, do we not know where we are at 1030? All we need to do to show our 1030 position is to move our 0930 position five miles in the direction of 045. The only slight problem is that we do not have a *single* position for the boat at 0930, we have a whole *set* of possibilities. Never mind: all we need do is move *all* the possibilities ahead the correct distance and direction and we then see where the boat must be at 1030: one of the points comprising a new line that is five miles northeast of the old one (Figure 10-10).

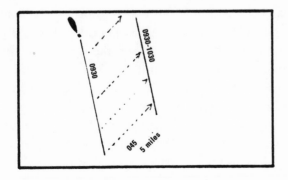

FIG. 10-10

Practically, this is done by choosing *any* point on the 0930 line as a representative point and plotting it ahead the correct distance and direction. Then the rest of the line is drawn through that point *parallel* to the original line. This is now an *advanced LOP* and must be labeled with *both* the time of its origin *and* the time to which it has been advanced (0930 to 1030). It is a set of possible positions for the boat at 1030 which is as accurate as our dead reckoning was between 0930 and 1030.

We still do not have that fix we were after and now it is 1030, but the lighthouse is still in sight, and because we have moved since 0930 its bearing has changed! If we take, plot and label a 1030 bearing of the lighthouse we discover that we have two intersecting LOPs which are valid for 1030 (Figure 10-11) and their intersection must be the position of the boat. This is our running fix.

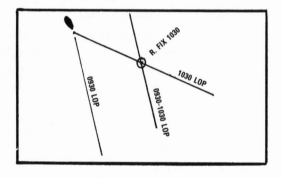

FIG. 10-11

Since the running fix is partially dependent on dead reckoning, it must be treated with more suspicion than a fix from two simultaneous LOPs, but usually the navigator has a fairly good sense of how good his DR will be over a relatively short period of time. It is regular practice in celestial navigation to use the sun at two different times of the day to obtain two separate LOPs. Then the earlier one is advanced to the time of the later for a running fix. Especially offshore, the possibility of a slight error due to DR is not significant.

This has been a look at the basic ideas of dead reckoning and piloting. The details are endless, and as numerous as there are navigators. Everyone has his favorite tricks, special techniques, and ways of organizing the job, and that means that the best advice to the student is to observe others in action and get all the practice possible. With the fundamental concepts in mind, the rest is common sense, a skeptical attitude, and no rest until the boat arrives at her destination!

CHAPTER ELEVEN

The Basis of Celestial Navigation

The most important thing to keep in mind in studying celestial navigation is its fundamental similarity to what we learned in piloting. We are again using a reference point to derive an LOP. Instead of lighthouses, buoys, and landmarks, however, we are looking to the sky and using the sun, moon, planets, and certain stars. But the process is the same: identify, locate, and then measure. Identification is either perfectly obvious as with the sun and moon, or a matter of becoming familiar with a few constellations and learning to recognize the important stars. There is no better time and place to do this than during night watches at sea.

We will limit this discussion of celestial navigation to the use of one reference point, the sun, partly because it is the easiest to observe, but also because once the process is understood for the sun it is a relatively simple matter to adapt it to the other bodies as the need and opportunity arise.

In piloting we related ourselves to a reference point by measuring its bearing or our distance from it. This measurement defined a set of points we called an LOP; a straight line in the first case and a circle in the second. Similarly, in celestial navigation we measure our "distance" from the sun and thereby define a circular LOP. However, the distance we measure is not distance in the sense of miles, but *angular distance,* as measured in degrees and minutes on the surface of a sphere. The sphere is the *celestial sphere,* the imaginary dome of the heavens that surrounds the earth and has its center at the center of the earth. The navigator's concept of astronomy places all the heavenly bodies on this sphere, and describes the distance between points on this sphere in terms of an angle with its vertex at the earth's center.

Since the earth and the celestial sphere share a common center, positions on the earth have corresponding positions on the celestial sphere and vice versa. Thus, when we look up and see the sun in a certain place in the sky, we can imagine a plumb bob on a string dropped from it to the surface of the earth indicating a corresponding position directly beneath the sun. Or if we tip our heads back and look *straight up* at the sky, we can imagine a point on the celestial sphere that is precisely above us. We call this point our *zenith,* and the sun's position on earth is called its *GP,* or *geographic position.*

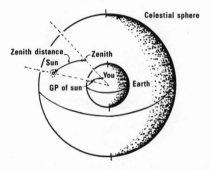

FIG. 11-1

If we could measure the angular distance between the sun and our zenith on the celestial sphere, or between ourselves and the sun's GP on earth, we would get the same number because they are arcs subtending the same angle at the earth's center (Figure 11-1). We call this arc the sun's *zenith distance.* A most convenient feature of a zenith distance is that although it is an angle and expressed in degrees and minutes, it is part of a great circle on the surface of the earth and therefore it can be readily converted into nautical miles by simply remembering that by definition a nautical mile is one minute of arc of a great circle.

What this means is that if we can measure the zenith distance of the sun, we can say how many miles we are from the sun's GP. Then, if we can find out where the sun's GP is, we know a great deal about where we are: we know that we are on a circular LOP with the sun's GP at its center and the zenith distance as its radius. Figure 11-2 illustrates this idea. If, for example, we have determined that there are 30° of arc between our zenith and the sun, then there are 30° of arc between us and the sun's GP, and that converts to 1,800 nautical miles (60 miles per degree). So we must be 1,800 miles from wherever the sun's GP is, and that defines a circle. It is very important to realize that we could be *anywhere* on this circular LOP and the zenith distance of the sun would still be 30°, but we must be on this line somewhere.

FIG. 11-2

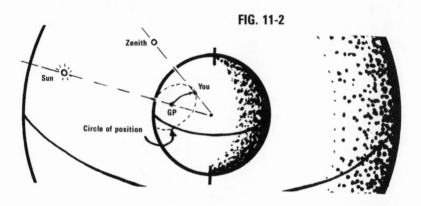

This is the basis for obtaining an LOP from a celestial body: measure the zenith distance between you and the body, convert the zenith distance to miles, and using it as the radius, draw a circle of position centered at the body's GP. There are only three things yet to be explained: (1) How do we know exactly where the GP of the sun is located at a given moment? (2) How do we measure the zenith distance between the sun and our zenith, which is invisible? And (3) how can we reasonably hope for any useful accuracy if we are plotting circles of position with radii of hundreds or thousands of miles? On a chart large enough to do this a pencil line would be many miles wide, and tiny errors would give rise to very inaccurate lines of position.

There is a very neat way around this third problem, which will be explained in Chapter 14, but first we must solve problems 1 and 2. In Chapter 12 we will learn to use an annual publication called the *Nautical Almanac,* which is simply a catalog of the predicted positions of the celestial bodies for every second of the year. From this we will obtain the precise position of the sun at the moment we observed it. In Chapter 13 we will learn how the marine *sextant* is used to measure—indirectly—the sun's zenith distance.

CHAPTER TWELVE

The Nautical Almanac

We have identified the celestial reference point that we will use as the sun, so the next step is to determine the location of the sun, just as in piloting we had to know the location of a buoy or lighthouse in order to derive an LOP from it. In order to talk about its position we must have a system of coordinates which we can use to describe locations of celestial bodies. Since these bodies are considered to be located on a sphere—the celestial sphere—it is reasonable to develop a system of coordinates similar to that used to describe positions on the earth, namely latitude and longitude. In fact, the system used on the celestial sphere is nearly identical.

Imagine a transparent earth with a light bulb at its center. The light would cause the earth's lines of latitude and longitude to be projected outward and onto the surrounding celestial sphere. They could then be used to describe the position of any celestial body in terms of its angular distance north or south of the *celestial equator,* and its angular distance east or west of the projection of the Greenwich meridian. There are only two differences between the system on earth and that on the celestial sphere. The first is names. Latitude on the celestial sphere is called *declination,* and longitude is called *Greenwich hour angle* (GHA). Declination works the same as latitude, that is, it starts with zero at the equator and increases to a maximum of 90° at either pole. Therefore, any expression of declination must include a north or south designation. GHA, like longitude, is measured from zero at Greenwich, but unlike longitude (and this is the second difference), it is only measured *west-*

ward, through 360°. Thus no designation of east or west is required—it is always west (see Figure 12-1).

With this coordinate system we can describe a position on the celestial sphere as accurately as we wish. Normally, for navigational purposes we will work to a tenth of a minute of angle. This is comparable to the accuracy we use with latitude and longitude on earth. Notice how easy it is to convert a celestial position to a geographic one. Suppose, for example, the sun was at this position on the celestial sphere:

Dec N 16°24.3' × GHA 125°53.7'.

The GP of the sun—its corresponding position on earth—is:

Lat 16°24.3' N × Long 125°53.7' W.

In the same way if our boat is at:

Lat 42°33.8' S × Long 158°30.6' E,

we can express the location of our zenith on the celestial sphere as:

Dec S 42°33.8' × GHA 201°29.4'.

Be sure to notice that since the longitude was *east,* it was necessary to *subtract* it from 360° to express GHA correctly. If that is not clear, take the time to study Figure 12-1 and do the subtraction.

FIG. 12-1

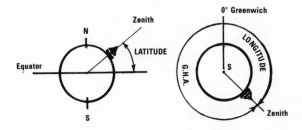

Unlike a lighthouse, the sun (and other celestial reference points) is not always in the same place. It is in constant motion, so in order to say where it is we must specify a *time*. In order to know precisely where the sun is *right now*, you would have to first know the time of "right now"—the year, month, day, hour, minute, and second. Since the sun's motion relative to the earth is regular, its position can be calculated and predicted, and this is what the *Nautical Almanac* does.

The sun's apparent movement around the earth, and therefore its position at any moment, is primarily the result of two things: the earth's orbit around the sun throughout the year, and the earth's rotation on its axis, once a day. Remember that the navigator sees the earth as standing still and the sun as moving. This means that the sun appears to travel from east to west throughout each day, and to migrate north and south throughout the year as a result of the earth's orbit and tilted axis (see Figure 12-2). It moves from about 23° north of the equator on June 21, to about 23° south of the equator on December 21, crossing the equator twice, once going north on March 21, and once going south on September 21. Thus if we are to know the sun's declination—how far north or south of the equator it is—we need only know the date and we can construct a simple graph that will tell us. It should be apparent that on a day-to-day basis the sun's declination changes, but very slowly.

FIG. 12-2

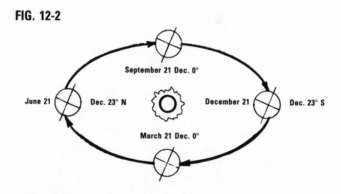

This is not the case with the sun's GHA, however. Its east-to-west motion results from the rotation of the earth on its axis, and we see the sun make a complete trip around the earth (360°) once a day. Since GHA is the measure of the sun's angular distance west of the Greenwich meridian, we can see that it is constantly increasing at the rate of 360° per day, starting over from zero every time the sun crosses the Greenwich meridian. To know the sun's GHA requires knowing the time of day, and since 360° per day means 15° per hour or 1° every four minutes, it is necessary to be very precise with time to locate a precise GHA.

We will be precise with time. When we make a celestial observation— "shoot the sun"—we will note the time to the nearest second on a reliable clock or watch, whose accuracy we check at frequent intervals. Clearly, any error in time will give us a false position for our reference point, which will simply be passed on as an error in our position.

Time, then, is the key to the sun's position. The *Nautical Almanac* catalogs its positions for the entire year, and to get at the information in the almanac, time is our key. There is one very important aspect of time that we must understand before we approach the almanac for information, and that is that the same moment is expressed differently in different parts of the world. For example, the moment when the sun's GHA is exactly 75° may be called 12 o'clock by you, and you eat lunch at this moment, but someone else in San Francisco is finishing breakfast and says this same moment is nine o'clock. If at this moment you both went to the almanac and looked up the sun's position for 12 o'clock and nine o'clock respectively, you would both get incorrect information. Either there would have to be 24 separate almanacs—one for each time zone—or we have to agree to use just one almanac and adjust our time accordingly. Obviously the latter is simpler in the long run and is what is done.

By tradition and international agreement, *Greenwich mean time* (GMT) is used as the standard. It is the time that is kept in the time zone whose center is at 0° longitude. The day begins there when the sun crosses longitude 180° at 2400/0000 hours, and it is 1200 when the sun crosses the Greenwich meridian (0° longitude). The *Nautical Almanac* is set up to be used *only* with GMT. This is not a problem as long as it is not forgotten or overlooked! It simply means that whenever we shoot the sun we must ask ourselves not just what time is it, but what time is it *in Greenwich* at this moment.

The difference between the time your watch says and the time in Greenwich will be a number of hours corresponding to the number of time zones you are east or west of Greenwich. Time changes one hour from one zone to the next. Each zone is 15° wide and has its center on a multiple of 15° longitude (Figure 12-3). Thus to determine the number of hours that your time differs from GMT, find out which 15° zone center is closest to you, divide that by 15, and apply that number of hours to your time—adding if you are west of Greenwich, subtracting if you are east. For example, on Cape Cod, the closest zone center is 75° W longitude, which is five hours away (75 ÷ 15) from Greenwich. Therefore when we are calling it 1200 hours (12 o'clock noon), it is 1700 GMT. To find the sun's position at this moment we would enter the almanac with 1700 GMT.

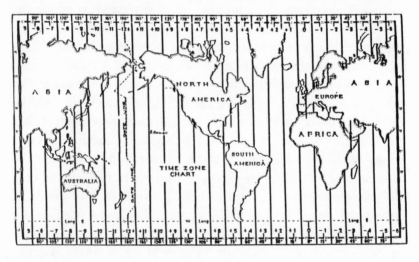

FIG. 12-3

At this same moment the person in California is calling it 0900. But to use the almanac he converts that time to GMT by noting that his nearest zone center is at 120° W longitude which is eight zones west of Greenwich. Adding eight hours to his time gives him the same GMT: 1700 hours.

In practice at sea we always know by how many hours our clocks differ from GMT because the boat's *chronometer* is kept set to GMT and checked daily by a radio time signal, which is given in GMT. When in doubt, however, the simple question to ask yourself is, "What time was it in Greenwich when I took my sight?"

With GMT in hand we can now go to the *Nautical Almanac* and look up the position of the sun. The main body of the almanac consists of the *daily pages,* printed on white paper. They contain the information we are looking for: the GHA and the declination of the sun. Figure 12-4 shows a pair of daily pages from the 1976 almanac for July 23, 24, and 25. Let us say we want to find out the position of the sun at exactly 15h 32m 46s GMT on July 23, 1976. This is the procedure:

(1) Open the almanac to the daily pages for July 23, and locate the vertical column that contains information about the sun. This will be on the right-hand page.

(2) On the left-hand edge of this page there are 24 hours given for each of the three days. Find 15 hours on the 23rd. It is helpful to lay a straight edge or piece of paper across the page under 15 hours to find the correct numbers in the next column.

(3) In the sun column, next to 15 hours, there are two numbers given. They are given in degrees, minutes, and tenths of a minute (see the symbols at the top of the column). These are the sun's GHA and declination respectively. Write them down, with labels, on your paper. Be sure to label the declination N or S, and notice that the degrees of declination are not printed every time.

We now know that at exactly 15 hours GMT on July 23, 1976, the sun was at:

GHA 43 23.7 and dec. N 19 58.0

(Just for practice, mentally convert that to latitude and longitude and picture where on earth the sun's GP is at that moment.)

However, we wanted to know the sun's position at 15h *32m 46s*. This is 32 minutes and 46 seconds later than 15 hours and the sun has not been standing still during that time. It has been moving westward, as it always does, at about 15° per hour, so we should expect to find that its GHA has increased by approximately 7.5 degrees. At this time of year (between June 21 and September 21) the sun is also moving slowly south, toward the equator, so we will

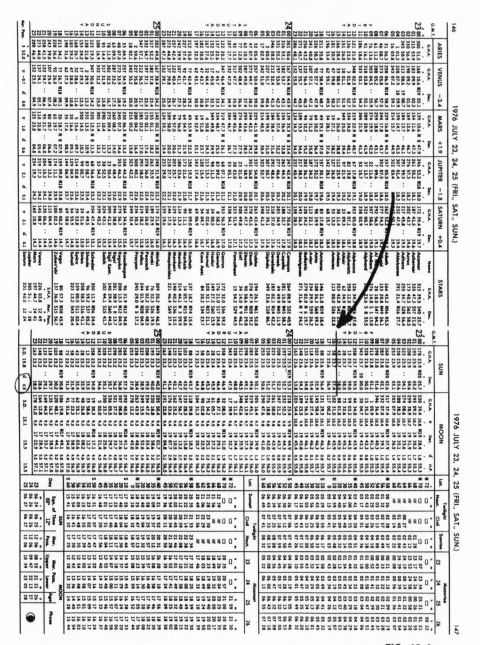

FIG. 12-4

32	SUN PLANETS	ARIES	MOON	v or Corr d	v or Corr d	v or Corr d
s	° '	° '	° '	' '	' '	' '
00	8 00·0	8 01·3	7 38·1	0·0 0·0	6·0 3·3	12·0 6·5
01	8 00·3	8 01·6	7 38·4	0·1 0·1	6·1 3·3	12·1 6·6
02	8 00·5	8 01·8	7 38·6	0·2 0·1	6·2 3·4	12·2 6·6
03	8 00·8	8 02·1	7 38·8	0·3 0·2	6·3 3·4	12·3 6·7
04	8 01·0	8 02·3	7 39·1	0·4 0·2	6·4 3·5	12·4 6·7
05	8 01·3	8 02·6	7 39·3	0·5 0·3	6·5 3·5	12·5 6·8
06	8 01·5	8 02·8	7 39·6	0·6 0·3	6·6 3·6	12·6 6·8
07	8 01·8	8 03·1	7 39·8	0·7 0·4	6·7 3·6	12·7 6·9
08	8 02·0	8 03·3	7 40·0	0·8 0·4	6·8 3·7	12·8 6·9
09	8 02·3	8 03·6	7 40·3	0·9 0·5	6·9 3·7	12·9 7·0
10	8 02·5	8 03·8	7 40·5	1·0 0·5	7·0 3·8	13·0 7·0
11	8 02·8	8 04·1	7 40·8	1·1 0·6	7·1 3·8	13·1 7·1
12	8 03·0	8 04·3	7 41·0	1·2 0·7	7·2 3·9	13·2 7·2
13	8 03·3	8 04·6	7 41·2	1·3 0·7	7·3 4·0	13·3 7·2
14	8 03·5	8 04·8	7 41·5	1·4 0·8	7·4 4·0	13·4 7·3
15	8 03·8	8 05·1	7 41·7	1·5 0·8	7·5 4·1	13·5 7·3
16	8 04·0	8 05·3	7 42·0	1·6 0·9	7·6 4·1	13·6 7·4
17	8 04·3	8 05·6	7 42·2	1·7 0·9	7·7 4·2	13·7 7·4
18	8 04·5	8 05·8	7 42·4	1·8 1·0	7·8 4·2	13·8 7·5
19	8 04·8	8 06·1	7 42·7	1·9 1·0	7·9 4·3	13·9 7·5
20	8 05·0	8 06·3	7 42·9	2·0 1·1	8·0 4·3	14·0 7·6
21	8 05·3	8 06·6	7 43·1	2·1 1·1	8·1 4·4	14·1 7·6
22	8 05·5	8 06·8	7 43·4	2·2 1·2	8·2 4·4	14·2 7·7
23	8 05·8	8 07·1	7 43·6	2·3 1·2	8·3 4·5	14·3 7·7
24	8 06·0	8 07·3	7 43·9	2·4 1·3	8·4 4·6	14·4 7·8
25	8 06·3	8 07·6	7 44·1	2·5 1·4	8·5 4·6	14·5 7·9
26	8 06·5	8 07·8	7 44·3	2·6 1·4	8·6 4·7	14·6 7·9
27	8 06·8	8 08·1	7 44·6	2·7 1·5	8·7 4·7	14·7 8·0
28	8 07·0	8 08·3	7 44·8	2·8 1·5	8·8 4·8	14·8 8·0
29	8 07·3	8 08·6	7 45·1	2·9 1·6	8·9 4·8	14·9 8·1
30	8 07·5	8 08·8	7 45·3	3·0 1·6	9·0 4·9	15·0 8·1
31	8 07·8	8 09·1	7 45·5	3·1 1·7	9·1 4·9	15·1 8·2
32	8 08·0	8 09·3	7 45·8	3·2 1·7	9·2 5·0	15·2 8·2
33	8 08·3	8 09·6	7 46·0	3·3 1·8	9·3 5·0	15·3 8·3
34	8 08·5	8 09·8	7 46·2	3·4 1·8	9·4 5·1	15·4 8·3
35	8 08·8	8 10·1	7 46·5	3·5 1·9	9·5 5·1	15·5 8·4
36	8 09·0	8 10·3	7 46·7	3·6 2·0	9·6 5·2	15·6 8·5
37	8 09·3	8 10·6	7 47·0	3·7 2·0	9·7 5·3	15·7 8·5
38	8 09·5	8 10·8	7 47·2	3·8 2·1	9·8 5·3	15·8 8·6
39	8 09·8	8 11·1	7 47·4	3·9 2·1	9·9 5·4	15·9 8·6
40	8 10·0	8 11·3	7 47·7	4·0 2·2	10·0 5·4	16·0 8·7
41	8 10·3	8 11·6	7 47·9	4·1 2·2	10·1 5·5	16·1 8·7
42	8 10·5	8 11·8	7 48·2	4·2 2·3	10·2 5·5	16·2 8·8
43	8 10·8	8 12·1	7 48·4	4·3 2·3	10·3 5·6	16·3 8·8
44	8 11·0	8 12·3	7 48·6	4·4 2·4	10·4 5·6	16·4 8·9
45	8 11·3	8 12·6	7 48·9	4·5 2·4	10·5 5·7	16·5 9·0
46	8 11·5	8 12·8	7 49·1	4·6 2·5	10·6 5·7	16·6 9·0
47	8 11·8	8 13·1	7 49·3	4·7 2·5	10·7 5·8	16·7 9·1
48	8 12·0	8 13·3	7 49·6	4·8 2·6	10·8 5·9	16·8 9·1
49	8 12·3	8 13·6	7 49·8	4·9 2·7	10·9 5·9	16·9 9·2
50	8 12·5	8 13·8	7 50·1	5·0 2·7	11·0 6·0	17·0 9·2
51	8 12·8	8 14·1	7 50·3	5·1 2·8	11·1 6·0	17·1 9·3
52	8 13·0	8 14·3	7 50·5	5·2 2·8	11·2 6·1	17·2 9·3
53	8 13·3	8 14·6	7 50·8	5·3 2·9	11·3 6·1	17·3 9·4
54	8 13·5	8 14·9	7 51·0	5·4 2·9	11·4 6·2	17·4 9·4
55	8 13·8	8 15·1	7 51·3	5·5 3·0	11·5 6·2	17·5 9·5
56	8 14·0	8 15·4	7 51·5	5·6 3·0	11·6 6·3	17·6 9·5
57	8 14·3	8 15·6	7 51·7	5·7 3·1	11·7 6·3	17·7 9·6
58	8 14·5	8 15·9	7 52·0	5·8 3·1	11·8 6·4	17·8 9·6
59	8 14·8	8 16·1	7 52·2	5·9 3·2	11·9 6·4	17·9 9·7
60	8 15·0	8 16·4	7 52·5	6·0 3·3	12·0 6·5	18·0 9·8

33	SUN PLANETS	ARIES	MOON	v or Corr d	v or Corr d	v or Corr d
s	° '	° '	° '	' '	' '	' '
00	8 15·0	8 16·4	7 52·5	0·0 0·0	6·0 3·4	12·0 6·7
01	8 15·3	8 16·6	7 52·7	0·1 0·1	6·1 3·4	12·1 6·8
02	8 15·5	8 16·9	7 52·9	0·2 0·1	6·2 3·5	12·2 6·8
03	8 15·8	8 17·1	7 53·2	0·3 0·2	6·3 3·5	12·3 6·9
04	8 16·0	8 17·4	7 53·4	0·4 0·2	6·4 3·6	12·4 6·9
05	8 16·3	8 17·6	7 53·6	0·5 0·3	6·5 3·6	12·5 7·0
06	8 16·5	8 17·9	7 53·9	0·6 0·3	6·6 3·7	12·6 7·0
07	8 16·8	8 18·1	7 54·1	0·7 0·4	6·7 3·7	12·7 7·1
08	8 17·0	8 18·4	7 54·4	0·8 0·4	6·8 3·8	12·8 7·1
09	8 17·3	8 18·6	7 54·6	0·9 0·5	6·9 3·9	12·9 7·2
10	8 17·5	8 18·9	7 54·8	1·0 0·6	7·0 3·9	13·0 7·3
11	8 17·8	8 19·1	7 55·1	1·1 0·6	7·1 4·0	13·1 7·3
12	8 18·0	8 19·4	7 55·3	1·2 0·7	7·2 4·0	13·2 7·4
13	8 18·3	8 19·6	7 55·6	1·3 0·7	7·3 4·1	13·3 7·4
14	8 18·5	8 19·9	7 55·8	1·4 0·8	7·4 4·1	13·4 7·5
15	8 18·8	8 20·1	7 56·0	1·5 0·8	7·5 4·2	13·5 7·5
16	8 19·0	8 20·4	7 56·3	1·6 0·9	7·6 4·2	13·6 7·6
17	8 19·3	8 20·6	7 56·5	1·7 0·9	7·7 4·3	13·7 7·6
18	8 19·5	8 20·9	7 56·7	1·8 1·0	7·8 4·4	13·8 7·7
19	8 19·8	8 21·1	7 57·0	1·9 1·1	7·9 4·4	13·9 7·8
20	8 20·0	8 21·4	7 57·2	2·0 1·1	8·0 4·5	14·0 7·8
21	8 20·3	8 21·6	7 57·5	2·1 1·2	8·1 4·5	14·1 7·9
22	8 20·5	8 21·9	7 57·7	2·2 1·2	8·2 4·6	14·2 7·9
23	8 20·8	8 22·1	7 57·9	2·3 1·3	8·3 4·6	14·3 8·0
24	8 21·0	8 22·4	7 58·2	2·4 1·3	8·4 4·7	14·4 8·0
25	8 21·3	8 22·6	7 58·4	2·5 1·4	8·5 4·7	14·5 8·1
26	8 21·5	8 22·9	7 58·7	2·6 1·5	8·6 4·8	14·6 8·2
27	8 21·8	8 23·1	7 58·9	2·7 1·5	8·7 4·9	14·7 8·2
28	8 22·0	8 23·4	7 59·1	2·8 1·6	8·8 4·9	14·8 8·3
29	8 22·3	8 23·6	7 59·4	2·9 1·6	8·9 5·0	14·9 8·3
30	8 22·5	8 23·9	7 59·6	3·0 1·7	9·0 5·0	15·0 8·4
31	8 22·8	8 24·1	7 59·8	3·1 1·7	9·1 5·1	15·1 8·4
32	8 23·0	8 24·4	8 00·1	3·2 1·8	9·2 5·1	15·2 8·5
33	8 23·3	8 24·6	8 00·3	3·3 1·8	9·3 5·2	15·3 8·5
34	8 23·5	8 24·9	8 00·6	3·4 1·9	9·4 5·2	15·4 8·6
35	8 23·8	8 25·1	8 00·8	3·5 2·0	9·5 5·3	15·5 8·7
36	8 24·0	8 25·4	8 01·0	3·6 2·0	9·6 5·4	15·6 8·7
37	8 24·3	8 25·6	8 01·3	3·7 2·1	9·7 5·4	15·7 8·8
38	8 24·5	8 25·9	8 01·5	3·8 2·1	9·8 5·5	15·8 8·8
39	8 24·8	8 26·1	8 01·8	3·9 2·2	9·9 5·5	15·9 8·9
40	8 25·0	8 26·4	8 02·0	4·0 2·2	10·0 5·6	16·0 8·9
41	8 25·3	8 26·6	8 02·2	4·1 2·3	10·1 5·6	16·1 9·0
42	8 25·5	8 26·9	8 02·5	4·2 2·3	10·2 5·7	16·2 9·0
43	8 25·8	8 27·1	8 02·7	4·3 2·4	10·3 5·8	16·3 9·1
44	8 26·0	8 27·4	8 02·9	4·4 2·5	10·4 5·8	16·4 9·2
45	8 26·3	8 27·6	8 03·2	4·5 2·5	10·5 5·9	16·5 9·2
46	8 26·5	8 27·9	8 03·4	4·6 2·6	10·6 5·9	16·6 9·3
47	8 26·8	8 28·1	8 03·7	4·7 2·6	10·7 6·0	16·7 9·3
48	8 27·0	8 28·4	8 03·9	4·8 2·7	10·8 6·0	16·8 9·4
49	8 27·3	8 28·6	8 04·1	4·9 2·7	10·9 6·1	16·9 9·4
50	8 27·5	8 28·9	8 04·4	5·0 2·8	11·0 6·1	17·0 9·5
51	8 27·8	8 29·1	8 04·6	5·1 2·8	11·1 6·2	17·1 9·5
52	8 28·0	8 29·4	8 04·9	5·2 2·9	11·2 6·3	17·2 9·6
53	8 28·3	8 29·6	8 05·1	5·3 3·0	11·3 6·3	17·3 9·7
54	8 28·5	8 29·9	8 05·3	5·4 3·0	11·4 6·4	17·4 9·7
55	8 28·8	8 30·1	8 05·6	5·5 3·1	11·5 6·4	17·5 9·8
56	8 29·0	8 30·4	8 05·8	5·6 3·1	11·6 6·5	17·6 9·8
57	8 29·3	8 30·6	8 06·1	5·7 3·2	11·7 6·5	17·7 9·9
58	8 29·5	8 30·9	8 06·3	5·8 3·2	11·8 6·6	17·8 9·9
59	8 29·8	8 31·1	8 06·5	5·9 3·3	11·9 6·6	17·9 10·0
60	8 30·0	8 31·4	8 06·8	6·0 3·4	12·0 6·7	18·0 10·1

xviii

FIG. 12-5

expect to find that even in a few minutes its declination has decreased slightly. These approximations are good exercise, but we need precision in this position, so we will use some tables which are provided for the purpose of accounting for the sun's change in position during these extra minutes and seconds of time.

(4) To correct the GHA for the 32m 46s, turn to the yellow pages at the back of the almanac called *Increments and Corrections*. Find the page with a box for 32m (see Figure 12-5). Find 46s in the left-hand column of the box and next to it, in the sun column, take out a correction of degrees, minutes, and tenths to be *added* to the GHA for 15 hours. This correction is always added because GHA always increases. This is the sun's exact GHA at our exact time.

(5) To correct the declination for the 32m 46s is easier because the declination changes less fast. Back on the daily page for July 23, at the same time that you wrote down the sun's declination at 15 hours, do two other things: (1) Notice whether declination is increasing or decreasing as time passes by looking on down the declination column, and (2) go to the bottom of the declination column and jot down the *d* code number there. In this case declination is *decreasing* and the code number is *d* 0.5. Now, when you are in the yellow pages and have finished with the GHA correction in the 32 minute box, take the *d* 0.5 to the columns in that box marked *v* or *d Corr*ⁿ. Search down the column until you find 0.5 and take out the number to the right of it. This is the correction to be made to the declination. It is small—usually only some tenths of a minute—and since you determined that declination is decreasing you will *subtract* it from the declination.

Your work should look like this:

for 15h:	GHA	43 23.7	Dec. N 19 58.0	(*d* 0.5)
Corrⁿ for 32m 46s:		+8 11.5	− 0.3	
	GHA	51 35.2	Dec. N 19 57.7	

That is it: we have located the exact position of our reference point at the moment we observed it. That sequence of steps in the almanac should be practiced until it is automatic. There are not many pitfalls other than careless arithmetic or misreading numbers from the tables. It is very important to remember that there are 60 minutes in a degree when adding and subtracting these numbers, especially when carrying and borrowing. And, of course, NEVER enter the almanac with anything but GMT!

CHAPTER THIRTEEN

The Sextant

Having identified and located our celestial reference point, it now remains to make some sort of measurement which will relate us to that point. While in piloting, this was most often a bearing taken with a compass, in celestial navigation we will be measuring an angle by means of a *sextant.*

The sextant is an optical instrument which measures the angle formed between two visible points and the observer's eye. It is generally capable of accuracy to a tenth of a minute. In celestial navigation the angle we will measure with the sextant is the angle of elevation of the celestial body we are using as a reference point above the horizon. We call this angle the *altitude* of the body, and sometimes refer to it as the *height* of the body above the horizon. It is always expressed in degrees, minutes, and tenths of a minute.

The modern sextant is descended from early angle-measuring tools such as the *astrolabe* and *cross-staff* shown in Figure 13-1. The astrolabe actually measured the zenith distance of the body directly, since it used gravity—the vertical—as its reference instead of the horizon. It is hard to imagine being able to use it on the deck of a rolling ship, however, and in any case for either of these instruments accuracy to within a whole degree would have been difficult. The deck of a rolling ship still is a challenge to the navigator, but with a little practice, accurate measurements can be made fairly easily with the modern sextant.

The task is to look at the horizon through an eyepiece—usually a telescope—and by adjusting a mirror, bring a reflected image of the

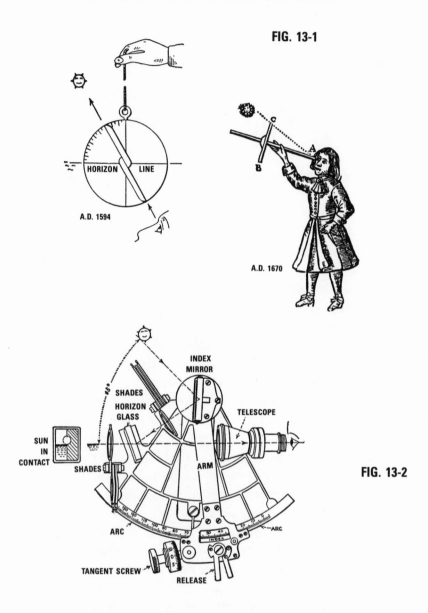

FIG. 13-1

HORIZON LINE

A.D. 1594

A.D. 1670

FIG. 13-2

INDEX MIRROR

SHADES

HORIZON GLASS

TELESCOPE

SUN IN CONTACT

SHADES

ARM

ARC

ARC

TANGENT SCREW

RELEASE

body into coincidence with it. The adjustment of the mirror is calibrated in degrees and read as the altitude of the body. Figure 13-2 shows how the sextant does this. The telescope looks straight at the *horizon glass,* which is vertically divided, half clear glass, half mirror. The horizon is viewed directly through the clear side, and beside it is seen the image of the celestial body which has been reflected twice: first by the *index mirror,* and then by the mirrored side of the horizon glass. The index mirror is adjusted by moving the *index arm* to which it is attached. When the index arm is moved back and forth, the image of the body in the telescope appears to rise and fall relative to the horizon. A precise measurement is made of the sun or moon by making either its upper or lower edge (*limb*) tangent to the horizon, and in the case of a star or planet by placing it exactly at the horizon line (Figure 13-3). Care and some practice are required to ensure that the measurement is being made *vertically* from the body to the horizon, because if it is the least bit off to one side the angle will be erroneously large.

The altitude is read from the sextant in two steps. Degrees are read from the *arc* directly over the indicating arrow on the arm. Then minutes and tenths of a minute are read on the *micrometer drum,* which is for fine-adjusting the reading. This drum is divided into 60 minutes, and usually provided with a vernier for reading tenths.

When we measure the altitude of the sun, although we are as careful as possible, there are several reasons why the angle the sextant gives us is not the true altitude of the sun. For navigational purposes we need the true altitude (*height observed,* abbreviated H_o) and a true altitude assumes among other things that our sextant is perfect, that we are standing at the center of the earth, and that we are measuring to the center of the sun. None of these is true, and so what we read directly off the sextant (abbreviated H_s, or *height by sextant*) is not useful until we have made some corrections to account for the discrepancies. We will look at these one at a time and arrive at a sequence of steps which we can use to correct sextant readings to true altitudes. We will need to do this for each sight we take.

The first thing we must take into account is whether or not the sextant itself is accurate. It may be, if it is a good quality instrument and is in good adjustment, but it is not safe to assume that it is perfect without first checking it. On the other hand, it is not necessary for the sextant to be perfect—most are not—as long as the amount by which it is in error is known. If the error is known, then it can be applied to any sights taken with the sextant and the result will be an accurate measurement. Error of this kind is called *index error* (I.E.).

Good practice is to check a sextant for index error each time it is used, because it is easy for a sextant to be knocked out of adjustment from careless handling. A good way to determine index error is to set the sextant to zero degrees, zero minutes, remove all filters, and look at the horizon. If there is no index error, the horizon seen through the clear glass and the horizon beside it in the mirror will form a continuous, unbroken line—the sextant is measuring an angle of zero. If there *is* index error, however, there will appear to be two horizons—the reflected one will be either above or below the real one, depending on whether the error is positive or negative.

If this is the case, the micrometer drum should be turned until the horizons are lined up as perfectly as possible in one straight line, and then the angle read on the drum. It should not amount to more than a few minutes of angle. (If it is much larger, the sextant's mirrors should be readjusted.) It must be noted whether the drum has moved the index arm *forward* (on the arc) from zero, or *backward* (off the arc) from zero. This tells us if we must add or subtract the error from subsequent readings to correct the sextant. The rule to remember is,

"If it's on, it's off; if it's off, it's on,"

which means that if the error is forward, on the arc, then it must be subtracted from any angle measured by the sextant, and vice versa.

This is the first correction made to H_s.

The next thing we must account for is the fact that the horizon we see is not really 90° from our zenith, or from the vertical, unless our eye is right at sea level. At sea level the horizon *is* tangent to the sea surface and at right angles to the vertical, but as our height of eye gets higher, the visible horizon dips lower and lower. The higher our eye, the bigger the amount of this *dip* angle. Figure 13-3 illustrates the situation. Dip is purely a function of our height of eye, so if that height is known, dip can be calculated. A table on the inside front cover of the Nautical Almanac provides the amount of dip to be subtracted from H_s for any height of eye. Simply determine height of eye at the time the sight is taken, find the corresponding dip angle in the table, and subtract it from H_s.

FIG. 13-3

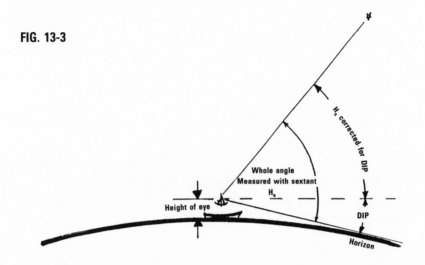

The resulting angle—H_s corrected for index error and dip—is called *apparent altitude*. Unfortunately this is still not the true altitude that we need. There are three more sources of error that we must allow for: *semidiameter, refraction,* and *parallax*. We will correct for all three of these errors by entering a single table with our apparent altitude, but we should know what each one is.

When we "shoot" the sun with the sextant, we actually measure from the horizon to either the upper or lower edge of the sun's disc. We would like to measure to its center, but nothing visible marks it. So for accuracy we use one edge and then add or subtract the angular measure of half the sun's apparent diameter (Figure 13-4). This is about 16′, but varies slightly as the earth's distance from the sun varies throughout the year. A correction for semidiameter must be made for observations of the moon, also, but stars and planets are considered to be points without diameter.

A correction for refraction accounts for the way light rays are bent as they enter the earth's atmosphere. The amount that they are bent depends on the angle at which they pass through the atmo-

FIG. 13-4

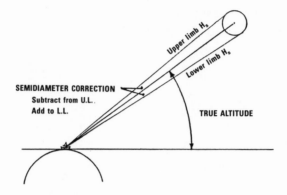

SEMIDIAMETER CORRECTION
Subtract from U.L.
Add to L.L.

TRUE ALTITUDE

Upper limb H_s

Lower limb H_s

sphere. In Figure 13-5 it is seen that the lower the sun is in the sky (i.e., the smaller the apparent altitude), the greater will be the error due to refraction. If the sun were directly overhead, there would be no refraction error.

FIG. 13-5   **FIG. 13-6**

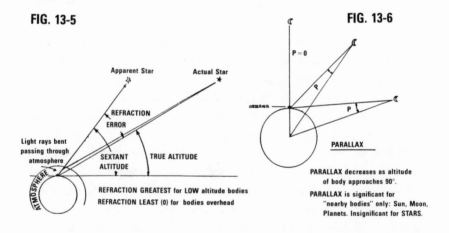

Apparent Star

Actual Star

REFRACTION ERROR

Light rays bent passing through atmosphere

SEXTANT ALTITUDE

TRUE ALTITUDE

REFRACTION GREATEST for LOW altitude bodies
REFRACTION LEAST (0) for bodies overhead

$P = 0$

OBSERVER

PARALLAX

PARALLAX decreases as altitude of body approaches 90°.

PARALLAX is significant for "nearby bodies" only: Sun, Moon, Planets. Insignificant for STARS.

Finally, in the case of the sun and the moon, which are relatively close to the earth, an error results from the fact that we are not standing at the center of the earth when we measure altitudes. The true altitude we need would have to be measured from the earth's center, but instead we can apply a correction that takes our distance from the center into account (Figure 13-6). This error is called parallax, and like refraction error, it is greatest for small angles of apparent altitude, and decreases to zero for a body directly over-head. Stars and planets are, for our purposes, infinitely far away, and therefore parallax error is insignificant for them.

Of these three sources of error, one is a constant and the other two are inversely related to apparent altitude. This allows for all three to be lumped together into a single table found inside the front cover of the almanac and called the Altitude Correction Table for the Sun. The table is entered first for the appropriate month, then for the apparent altitude, and the total correction is taken out from the Upper Limb or Lower Limb column depending on which way the sun was observed. The correction is a number of minutes of angle and is added to or subtracted from the apparent altitude. The result of this is now the true altitude of the sun, called the height observed, or H_o. This corrected altitude of the sun above the horizon, if subtracted from 90°, would give us the exact zenith distance of the sun at the moment we took the sight. We will use this H_o in calculating a line of position.

CHAPTER FOURTEEN

The Plotting Problem
and a Solution:
The Assumed Position

With no more than the information we now have, and with a globe or world chart on which to plot, we can determine our whereabouts by the sun. We can measure the sun's altitude and note the time. We can correct the sextant reading to be a true altitude (H_o), and by converting our local time to GMT we can then use it to find the exact location of the sun from the almanac. Although the almanac gives us the sun's celestial coordinates, it is no problem to convert them to latitude and longitude and then we can plot the sun's GP on our globe. Now, if we subtract our H_o from 90° we will have the zenith distance of the sun — the angle between it and the point directly over our head. On the earth this angle can be converted into nautical miles, so the zenith distance actually tells us how many miles we are from the sun's GP. If we are a known number of miles from a known point, we are entitled to draw a circle around that point whose radius is that number of miles and assume that we must be on the circle. The circle is an LOP, as valid as any obtained from a bearing on a lighthouse, or distance-off by radar.

Of course, we do not have a *fix*. We still need another LOP to cross this one to give us a fix, but that is easily obtained by waiting until the sun has moved to another part of the sky and then taking another sight. This will produce another circular LOP which will intersect the first one, and there is the fix (or *running fix;* if we have been moving we will have to advance the earlier LOP to make a valid intersection).

The procedure outlined above is not an oversimplification in theory, but it does run into a practical problem in the plotting stage. The problem is that the GPs of the celestial bodies are apt to be all over the globe, often thousands of miles from our position, so that to plot these GPs and ourselves at the same time would require the use of a huge chart or even a globe. It would not only be impractical to try to navigate our boat on the curved surface of a globe, but the scale would be such that even with very careful work we could not hope for much accuracy. A pencil line would be ten or twenty miles wide! Our sextant reads to a tenth of a minute and the almanac gives us the sun's position to tenths of a minute, so we should be able to get LOP's that are accurate to tenths of a mile. We need a means of "localizing" the plotting.

What follows is a solution to this plotting problem. It is basically a simple piece of logic, but it involves several steps, some new terms and another book of tables. As we work through this explanation, it is important not to lose sight of the underlying idea as stated in the first paragraph of this chapter, and remember we are now just trying to make the plotting reasonable!

Imagine standing in a vast field which is empty except for a tall flagpole some distance away from us. The flagpole's height is known and its position in the field is known. We have a general idea of where we are (sort of a DR position) but would like to get an accurate LOP. We have a sextant.

By measuring the angle between the base and the top of the flagpole—and knowing its height—we can use trigonometry to calculate our distance from the pole (Figure 14-1). With this distance as a radius we can draw a circular LOP and know that we are on it. But there is a plotting problem—we do not want to plot on a huge map of the whole field.

Let's take a slightly different approach. Before taking out our

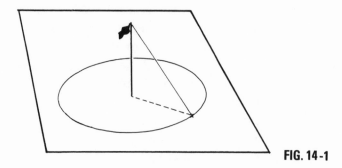

FIG. 14-1

sextant and measuring the height of the flagpole, let's play "just suppose." We have some general idea of our whereabouts (and even if it is not close it will not matter), so let's *assume* that we are in a particular spot—just pick a point, mark it on our map, and pretend for the moment that we are there. If we were really at this point, since the height and position of the flagpole are known, we would be able to compute in reverse what the angle is between the base and the top of the pole. In other words, we work the same triangle problem backwards. Knowing the height of the flagpole and the distance between its base and this *assumed position* (AP) we can calculate the angle of elevation and say, "*If* we were there, the angle would be, for example, 50°."

Now we take out the sextant and actually measure the angle. It comes as no surprise that the real angle is different from the one we computed because we knew all along that we were not really at that assumed position. But think about what the difference tells us. Let's say the real (observed) angle is 51°10′. In the first place, the fact that it is *greater* than the computed angle tells us that we must be *closer* to the flagpole than if we had been at the AP. (Be sure the logic of this is understood: if you walked *toward* the pole you would have to look further and further *up* to see the flag, and, of course, the reverse would be true if you walked away).

In the second place, the *amount* by which it is greater tells us *how much* closer we are. If it so happens that in this field a mile equals a minute of angle, then we can say that we are 10 miles closer to the flagpole than if we had been at the assumed position. To plot this, we draw a circle around the pole whose radius is 10 miles less than the distance to the AP. This circle is then the LOP resulting from our sextant measurement.

This apparently roundabout process of coming up with the same LOP as before has one very important feature. There is no need to show the flagpole on the map at all. Figure 14-2 is a local map of the part of the field where we are.

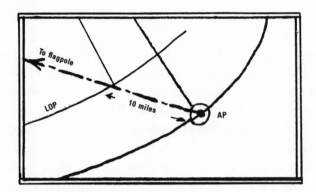

FIG. 14-2

On this local map we have plotted the assumed position. Even though the flagpole is too far away to appear on this map, we can indicate the direction in which the flagpole lies from that point. But now that we know that we are somewhere 10 miles closer to the pole than the assumed position, we can plot this fact by measuring 10 miles toward the pole and constructing through that point a line perpendicular to the direction of the pole. On a local scale we can draw this as a straight line, but in fact it is a piece of the huge circular LOP around the distant flagpole. We are somewhere on it.

It may be tempting to jump to the conclusion that we are at a particular point on the LOP—where it crosses the line pointing toward the flagpole. *There is nothing special about that point.* All we know for certain from our one sight is that we are *somewhere* on the LOP.

It works just the same way with the celestial bodies and the earth. By computing how high and in what direction the sun *would be* if we were at an assumed position, and comparing that height to the height we actually observe with a sextant, we can plot ourselves on an LOP not far from the assumed position — the LOP being a part of a very large circle of position. The system will work no matter how far away our AP may be from our true position. If it is very far away we will find a large difference between the computed and the observed heights, and the plotting again begins to get impractical. However, at sea we will usually have a good enough idea of where we are from our DR, even if we have been sailing for several days without a fix.

In order to use this method, then, what we require is to be able to calculate how high and in what direction the sun would appear to us if we were at an assumed position. Intuitively, it should seem reasonable that if we know where in the sky the sun is (from the almanac) and we know where we are looking from (an AP), then the sun's altitude and bearing should be calculable. It is like saying we know the address and the height of the Empire State Building, and we know we are at Broadway and 42nd Street, so there should be a way of figuring out how high up to look and in what direction to see the top of the building. The method is simple if we picture everything on the celestial sphere, and if we recall a theorem from geometry which says that if you know two sides and the included angle of a triangle, then you can calculate the other angles and side.

Figure 14-3 shows the sun and the zenith of an assumed position as forming two corners of a triangle on the celestial sphere, with the north pole making the third corner. One side of this triangle, the side labelled *zenith distance,* is of great interest to us because subtracted from 90° it would tell us the altitude (H_o) of the sun as seen from the assumed position. If we know the length of this side we can easily know the sun's *computed altitude.* Computed altitude is abbreviated H_c. Let us look at the rest of the triangle and see what we may know about its other parts.

One of its other two sides is the distance from the sun to the north celestial pole. Since we know the coordinates of the sun's position from the almanac, we know how far the sun is north of the equator. So by simply subtracting the sun's declination from 90° we know the length of this side.

The other side is the distance from the AP to the north pole. Since

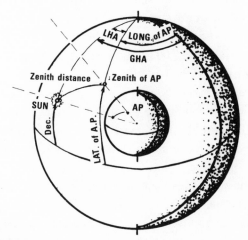

FIG. 14-3

the coordinates of the assumed position are known (we *chose* them) we can in a similar way find the length of this side by subtracting the latitude of the AP from 90°.

We have two sides known. If we knew—or could find out—the angle between them we could "solve the triangle." This included angle is the one with its vertex at the north pole, and can be described as the *longitude difference* between the sun and the AP. The longitude of the assumed position is whatever we chose it to be—something close to our DR. The sun's longitude (its GHA) is found in the almanac. It should be apparent from Figure 14-3 that if the longitude of the assumed position were subtracted from the sun's GHA, we would be left with the angle in question.

This angle is given the name *local hour angle* (LHA). It is like GHA in that it is an angular measurement to the *west*, but instead of using the Greenwich meridian as a starting point, we start measuring LHA *locally*—that is, in this case, at the meridian of the AP.

Thus it turns out that by knowing the coordinates of the sun and the coordinates of an assumed position we know two sides and the included angle of a triangle, and that is sufficient "input" for a trig table to solve the triangle and tell us any of the remaining parts we would like to know. Specifically, we would like to know the length of the zenith distance side so that we can subtract it from 90° and find out what the H_c of the sun would be if we were at AP. Also we will need to know the angle between the zenith distance side and north—the angle labelled Z. That will tell us the *direction* in which the sun lies from the AP.

With this information we can go to our local chart, plot the assumed position and show the direction to the sun from it. Then by comparing H_c and H_o (what we actually *observe*) we can place our LOP either closer to the sun or farther away from the sun by the amount of the difference.

In a sense, the AP serves as a secondary reference point. Where the primary reference point—the sun's GP—is too far away for practicality in plotting, we set up a secondary one with a known relationship to the first, and then relate ourselves to that by comparing the actually observed height to the hypothetically calculated height.

If the purpose of the exercise is now clear, it only remains to learn how to find the H_c and Z for a given AP and position of the sun. This is simply a mechanical matter of using a trig table that has been specially set up to solve this navigational triangle, and is the subject of the next chapter.

CHAPTER FIFTEEN

H.O. 249

Many tables called "sight reduction tables" exist for the purpose of solving the particular trig problem described in the previous chapter. Which one to use is mostly a matter of personal preference. We will use the table known as *H.O. 249*, which simply stands for Hydrographic Office publication number 249. The table can be thought of as a computer which takes input and generates output. The input in this case consists of the two sides and the included angle of our triangle. From this the table will solve the triangle and give us back the information we need: H_c and Z.

For convenience, the table is arranged so that we do not need to subtract anything from 90° before entering. Therefore we enter the table with (1) the latitude of our assumed position, (2) the declination of the sun, and (3) the LHA between the AP and the sun. The table then tells us (1) H_c, the computed height of the sun from the AP (zenith distance already subtracted from 90°), and (2) Z, the bearing of the sun from the AP.

In exchange for this convenience, however, the table makes a few demands. The first of these is that the latitude of the AP must be a whole number of degrees, with no minutes or tenths. That is no problem since we are free to choose any AP we want anyway. We will just choose an AP which lies on a whole degree of latitude.

The second is that LHA must also be a whole number of degrees. This requires a bit more attention. Remember that LHA is the angular distance that the sun is *west* of the AP. In practice it is found by *subtracting* the longitude of the AP from the sun's GHA *when the assumed longitude is west,* or by *adding* the assumed longitude to GHA *when it is east.* The diagrams in Figure 15-1 illustrate this. Since we are free to choose any longitude we like for AP, we can choose a longitude whose minutes and tenths combine with those of the GHA in such a way as to disappear and leave only whole degrees in the resulting LHA.

For example, in the left-hand diagram of Figure 15-1, the sun's GHA is 62°12.3′ and the AP is going to be near 40°W longitude. To find LHA we will be subtracting the assumed longitude from the GHA, so let's choose an assumed longitude of 40°12.3′. Then, when we subtract it from 62°12.3′, we are left with an LHA of 22°. In east longitude the minutes would have to be chosen to *add* together with the minutes of the GHA to produce a whole degree.

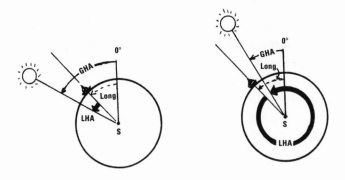

FIG. 15-1

Notice in the right-hand diagram the assumed longitude is greater than the GHA. In order to be able to subtract it, 360° must first be added to the GHA. By the same token, in east longitude the result of adding assumed longitude and GHA together may end up greater than 360°, in which case 360° must then be subtracted from the result.

The final demand made by the table is that we must decide for ourselves whether the sun is east or west of the AP. The angle Z, called the *azimuth* of the sun, tells us only that it is so many degrees from north, but not which side of north. If we learn that Z is 120°

this can mean either that the sun lies 120° *east* of north (which by a compass would be called a bearing of 120°), or that it lies 120° *west* of north (and this, by compass, would be called 360 minus 120°, or 240°). All we really need to know to resolve this ambiguity for the sun is whether it is morning or afternoon. In the morning the sun is east of your longitude, and in the afternoon it is west of it. So for any observation of the sun done in the morning the number given for Z can be plotted directly as a true bearing. For afternoon sights, however, that Z number must be subtracted from 360° before it can be plotted as a bearing. The rules for correct treatment of Z are given on each page of the table for easy reference!

Volume I of *H.O. 249* is exclusively for stars and is not covered here. We will use volumes II and III, which are good for any latitude from 0° to 89° north or south and for declinations from 0° to 29° north or south. The procedure is as follows (refer to the sample page in Figure 15-2):

We have "shot the sun"—measured its altitude and taken the time.

We have corrected our sextant reading from H_s to H_o.

We have looked up the sun's GHA and declination in the almanac.

We have chosen an AP so that its latitude is a whole degree, and its longitude combines with the GHA to produce an LHA in whole degrees.

Enter *H.O. 249* with the *assumed latitude* first, finding that there are several pages for each whole degree of latitude.

Using the *degrees* of the sun's declination, find the appropriate vertical column on the appropriate page. There is a column for each degree of declination, and we are asked whether the declination and the assumed latitude have *same* or *contrary* names—that is, are they both north or both south, or is one north and the other south? Once that is sorted out and we are in the correct column, look up and down each side until the LHA is found.

Write down the H_c, the Z, and the small number labelled *d*, with its sign. Decide whether Z needs to be subtracted from 360° for an afternoon sight or left as is for a morning sight, and when it is ready to plot, label it Zn.

FIG. 15-2

N. Lat. {LHA greater than 180° ...... Zn=Z; LHA less than 180° ...... Zn=360−Z}

DECLINATION (0°-14°) CONTRARY NAME TO LATITUDE — LAT 33°

LHA	0° Hc	d	Z	1° Hc	d	Z	2° Hc	d	Z	3° Hc	d	Z	4° Hc	d	Z	5° Hc	d	Z	6° Hc	d	Z	7° Hc	d	Z
	° ′	′	°	° ′	′	°	° ′	′	°	° ′	′	°	° ′	′	°	° ′	′	°	° ′	′	°	° ′	′	°
69	17 29	34	102	16 55	34	103	16 21	35	104	15 46	35	104	15 11	35	105	14 36	36	106	14 00	35	107	13 25	36	108
68	18 19	35	102	17 44	35	103	17 09	35	104	16 34	35	105	15 59	35	106	15 24	36	107	14 48	35	108	14 13	36	108
67	19 08	35	103	18 33	35	104	17 58	35	105	17 23	35	106	16 48	36	106	16 12	36	107	15 36	36	109	15 00	36	109
66	19 57	35	104	19 22	35	105	18 47	36	105	18 11	35	106	17 36	36	107	17 00	36	108	16 24	36	109	15 48	37	110
65	20 46	−35	104	20 11	−36	105	19 35	−35	106	19 00	−36	107	18 24	−36	108	17 48	−36	109	17 12	−37	109	16 35	−37	110
64	21 34	35	105	20 59	36	106	20 23	35	107	19 48	36	108	19 12	37	108	18 35	36	109	17 59	37	110	17 22	37	111
63	22 23	36	106	21 47	35	106	21 12	36	107	20 36	37	108	19 59	36	109	19 23	37	110	18 46	37	111	18 09	37	112
62	23 11	35	106	22 36	36	107	22 00	37	108	21 23	36	109	20 47	37	110	20 10	37	110	19 33	37	111	18 56	38	112
61	24 00	36	107	23 24	37	108	22 47	36	109	22 11	37	109	21 34	37	110	20 57	37	111	20 20	38	112	19 42	37	113
60	24 48	−37	108	24 11	−36	108	23 35	−37	109	22 58	−37	110	22 21	−37	111	21 44	−38	112	21 06	−37	113	20 29	−38	113
59	25 36	37	108	24 59	37	109	24 22	37	110	23 45	37	111	23 08	37	112	22 31	38	112	21 53	38	113	21 15	39	114
58	26 23	36	109	25 47	37	110	25 10	38	111	24 32	37	111	23 55	38	112	23 17	38	113	22 39	38	114	22 01	39	115
57	27 11	37	110	26 34	37	110	25 57	38	111	25 19	38	112	24 41	38	113	24 03	38	114	23 25	39	115	22 46	39	116
56	27 58	37	110	27 21	38	111	26 43	37	112	26 06	38	113	25 28	39	114	24 49	39	115	24 10	39	115	23 31	39	116
55	28 45	−37	111	28 08	−38	112	27 30	−38	113	26 52	−39	114	26 13	−38	114	25 35	−39	115	24 56	−40	116	24 16	−39	117
54	29 32	38	112	28 54	38	113	28 16	38	113	27 38	39	114	26 59	39	115	26 20	39	116	25 41	40	117	25 01	40	118
53	30 19	38	112	29 41	39	113	29 02	38	114	28 24	39	115	27 45	40	116	27 05	39	117	26 26	40	118	25 46	41	118
52	31 05	38	113	30 27	39	114	29 48	39	115	29 09	39	116	28 30	40	117	27 50	40	117	27 10	40	118	26 30	41	119
51	31 51	38	114	31 13	39	115	30 34	40	116	29 54	39	117	29 15	40	117	28 35	41	118	27 54	40	119	27 14	41	120
50	32 37	−39	115	31 58	−39	116	31 19	−40	116	30 39	−40	117	29 59	−40	118	29 19	−41	119	28 38	−41	120	27 57	−41	121
49	33 23	39	115	32 44	40	116	32 04	40	117	31 24	41	118	30 43	40	119	30 03	41	120	29 22	42	121	28 40	42	121
48	34 08	39	116	33 29	40	117	32 49	41	118	32 08	41	119	31 27	41	120	30 46	41	121	30 05	42	121	29 23	42	122
47	34 53	40	117	34 13	40	118	33 33	41	119	32 52	41	120	32 11	42	121	31 29	41	121	30 48	43	122	30 05	42	123
46	35 38	40	118	34 58	41	119	34 17	41	120	33 36	42	120	32 54	42	121	32 12	42	122	31 30	43	123	30 47	43	124
45	36 22	−40	119	35 42	−42	120	35 00	−41	120	34 19	−42	121	33 37	−42	122	32 55	−43	123	32 12	−43	124	31 29	−43	125
44	37 06	41	119	36 25	41	120	35 44	42	121	35 02	43	122	34 19	42	123	33 37	43	124	32 54	44	125	32 10	43	126
43	37 50	42	120	37 08	42	121	36 26	42	122	35 44	43	123	35 01	43	124	34 18	43	125	33 35	44	126	32 51	44	126
42	38 33	42	121	37 51	42	122	37 09	43	123	36 26	43	124	35 43	44	125	34 59	44	126	34 15	44	126	33 31	44	127
41	39 16	42	122	38 34	43	123	37 51	43	124	37 08	44	125	36 24	44	126	35 40	44	126	34 56	45	127	34 11	45	128
40	39 59	−43	123	39 16	−44	124	38 32	−43	125	37 49	−44	126	37 05	−45	127	36 20	−44	127	35 36	−46	128	34 50	−45	129
39	40 41	44	124	39 57	43	125	39 14	45	126	38 29	44	127	37 45	45	127	37 00	45	128	36 15	46	129	35 29	45	130
38	41 22	44	125	40 38	44	126	39 54	44	127	39 10	45	128	38 25	46	128	37 39	45	129	36 54	46	130	36 08	47	131
37	42 03	44	126	41 19	45	127	40 34	45	128	39 49	45	129	39 04	46	129	38 18	46	130	37 32	47	131	36 45	46	132
36	42 44	45	127	41 59	45	128	41 14	46	129	40 28	46	130	39 42	46	130	38 56	46	131	38 10	47	132	37 23	47	133
35	43 24	−46	128	42 38	−45	129	41 53	−46	130	41 07	−47	131	40 20	−46	131	39 34	−47	132	38 47	−48	133	37 59	−47	134
34	44 03	46	129	43 17	46	130	42 31	46	131	41 45	47	132	40 58	47	132	40 11	48	133	39 23	48	134	38 35	48	135
33	44 42	46	130	43 56	47	131	43 09	47	132	42 22	47	133	41 35	48	133	40 47	48	134	39 59	48	135	39 11	49	136
32	45 20	47	131	44 33	47	132	43 46	47	133	42 59	48	134	42 11	48	135	41 23	49	135	40 34	48	136	39 46	50	137
31	45 58	47	132	45 11	48	133	44 23	48	134	43 35	48	135	42 47	49	136	41 58	49	136	41 09	49	137	40 20	50	138
30	46 35	−48	133	45 47	−48	134	44 59	−49	135	44 10	−48	136	43 22	−50	137	42 32	−49	138	41 43	−50	138	40 53	−50	139
29	47 11	48	135	46 23	49	135	45 34	49	136	44 45	49	137	43 56	50	138	43 06	50	139	42 16	50	139	41 26	51	140
28	47 47	49	136	46 58	50	137	46 08	49	137	45 19	50	138	44 29	50	139	43 39	51	140	42 48	50	141	41 58	51	141
27	48 21	49	137	47 32	50	138	46 42	50	139	45 52	50	139	45 02	51	140	44 11	51	141	43 20	51	142	42 29	52	142
26	48 55	50	138	48 05	50	139	47 15	51	140	46 24	50	141	45 34	52	141	44 42	51	142	43 51	52	143	42 59	52	144
25	49 28	−50	139	48 38	−51	140	47 47	−51	141	46 56	−51	142	46 05	−52	143	45 13	−52	143	44 21	−52	144	43 29	−53	145
24	50 01	51	141	49 10	52	142	48 18	51	142	47 27	52	143	46 35	53	144	45 42	52	145	44 50	53	145	43 57	53	146
23	50 32	51	142	49 41	52	143	48 49	53	144	47 56	52	144	47 04	53	145	46 11	53	146	45 18	53	147	44 25	53	147
22	51 03	53	143	50 10	52	144	49 18	53	145	48 25	53	146	47 32	53	146	46 39	53	147	45 46	54	148	44 52	54	148
21	51 32	53	145	50 39	53	146	49 46	53	146	48 53	53	147	48 00	54	148	47 06	54	148	46 12	54	149	45 18	55	150
20	52 01	−54	146	51 07	−53	147	50 14	−54	148	49 20	−54	148	48 26	−54	149	47 32	−55	150	46 37	−54	150	45 43	−55	151
19	52 28	54	148	51 34	54	148	50 40	54	149	49 46	55	150	48 51	54	150	47 57	55	151	47 02	55	152	46 07	55	152
18	52 54	54	149	52 00	55	150	51 05	54	151	50 11	55	151	49 16	55	152	48 21	56	152	47 25	55	153	46 30	56	154
17	53 19	54	151	52 25	55	151	51 30	56	152	50 34	55	153	49 39	56	153	48 43	55	154	47 48	56	154	46 52	56	155
16	53 44	56	152	52 48	55	153	51 53	56	154	50 57	56	154	50 01	56	155	49 05	56	155	48 09	57	156	47 12	56	156
15	54 06	−55	154	53 11	−56	154	52 15	−57	155	51 18	−56	156	50 22	−57	156	49 25	−56	157	48 29	−57	157	47 32	−57	158
14	54 28	56	155	53 32	57	156	52 35	56	157	51 39	57	157	50 42	57	158	49 45	57	158	48 48	57	159	47 51	58	159
13	54 48	57	157	53 51	56	158	52 55	58	158	51 57	57	159	51 00	57	159	50 03	57	160	49 06	58	160	48 08	57	161
12	55 07	57	159	54 10	57	159	53 13	58	160	52 15	57	160	51 18	58	161	50 20	58	161	49 22	58	162	48 24	58	162
11	55 25	58	160	54 27	58	161	53 29	57	161	52 32	58	162	51 34	58	162	50 36	58	163	49 38	59	163	48 39	58	163
10	55 41	−58	162	54 43	−58	163	53 45	−58	163	52 47	−59	163	51 48	−58	164	50 50	−58	164	49 52	−59	165	48 53	−58	165
9	55 56	59	164	54 57	58	164	53 59	59	165	53 00	58	165	52 02	59	165	51 03	58	166	50 05	59	166	49 06	59	166
8	56 09	59	166	55 10	58	166	54 12	59	166	53 13	59	167	52 14	59	167	51 15	59	167	50 16	59	168	49 17	59	168
7	56 21	59	167	55 22	59	168	54 23	59	168	53 24	59	168	52 25	60	169	51 25	59	169	50 26	59	169	49 27	59	169
6	56 31	59	169	55 32	59	169	54 33	60	170	53 33	59	170	52 34	59	170	51 35	60	170	50 35	59	171	49 36	60	171
5	56 40	−59	171	55 41	−60	171	54 41	−60	171	53 41	−59	172	52 42	−60	172	51 42	−59	172	50 43	−60	172	49 43	−59	172
4	56 47	59	173	55 48	60	173	54 48	60	173	53 48	60	173	52 48	59	173	51 49	60	174	50 49	60	174	49 49	60	174
3	56 53	60	175	55 53	60	175	54 53	60	175	53 53	59	175	52 54	60	175	51 54	60	175	50 54	60	175	49 54	60	175
2	56 57	60	176	55 57	60	126	54 57	60	177	53 57	60	177	52 57	60	177	51 57	60	177	50 57	60	177	49 57	60	177
1	56 59	60	178	55 59	60	178	54 59	60	178	53 59	60	178	52 59	60	178	51 59	60	178	50 59	60	178	49 59	60	179
0	57 00	−60	180	56 00	−60	180	55 00	−60	180	54 00	−60	180	53 00	−60	180	52 00	−60	180	51 00	−60	180	50 00	−60	180

LHA	8° Hc	d	Z	9° Hc	d	Z	10° Hc	d	Z	11° Hc	d	Z	12° Hc	d	Z	13° Hc	d	Z	14° Hc	d	Z	LHA
	° ′	′	°	° ′	′	°	° ′	′	°	° ′	′	°	° ′	′	°	° ′	′	°	° ′	′	°	
69	12 49	36	109	12 13	36	109	11 37	36	110	11 01	36	111	10 25	37	112	09 48	36	113	09 12	37	113	291
68	13 37	36	109	13 01	37	110	12 24	36	111	11 48	37	112	11 11	36	112	10 35	37	113	09 58	37	114	292
67	14 24	36	110	13 48	37	111	13 11	36	111	12 35	37	112	11 58	37	113	11 21	37	114	10 44	37	115	293
66	15 11	36	110	14 35	37	111	13 58	37	112	13 21	37	113	12 44	37	114	12 07	37	114	11 30	38	115	294
65	15 58	−36	111	15 22	−37	112	14 45	−38	113	14 07	−37	114	13 30	−37	114	12 53	−38	115	12 15	−38	116	295
64	16 45	37	112	16 08	37	113	15 31	38	113	14 53	37	114	14 16	38	115	13 38	38	116	13 00	38	117	296
63	17 32	37	112	16 55	38	113	16 17	38	114	15 39	38	115	15 01	38	116	14 23	38	116	13 45	38	117	297
62	18 18	37	113	17 41	38	114	17 03	38	115	16 25	38	115	15 47	39	116	15 08	38	117	14 30	39	118	298
61	19 05	38	114	18 27	38	114	17 49	39	115	17 10	38	116	16 32	39	117	15 53	39	118	15 14	39	118	299
60	19 51	−39	114	19 12	−38	115	18 34	−39	116	17 55	−39	117	17 16	−39	118	16 37	−39	118	15 58	−39	119	300
59	20 36	38	115	19 58	39	116	19 19	39	117	18 40	39	117	18 01	39	118	17 22	40	119	16 42	40	120	301
58	21 22	39	116	20 43	39	116	20 04	39	117	19 25	40	118	18 45	40	119	18 05	39	120	17 26	41	120	302
57	22 07	39	116	21 28	39	117	20 49	40	118	20 09	40	119	19 29	40	120	18 49	40	120	18 09	41	121	303
56	22 52	39	117	22 13	40	118	21 33	40	119	20 53	40	119	20 13	41	120	19 32	40	121	18 52	41	122	304
55	23 37	−40	118	22 57	−40	119	22 17	−40	119	21 37	−41	120	20 56	−41	121	20 15	−41	122	19 34	−41	123	305
54	24 21	40	118	23 41	40	119	23 01	41	120	22 20	41	121	21 39	41	122	20 58	41	122	20 17	42	123	306
53	25 05	40	119	24 25	41	120	23 44	41	121	23 03	41	122	22 22	42	122	21 40	41	123	20 59	42	124	307
52	25 49	41	120	25 08	41	121	24 27	41	122	23 46	42	122	23 04	42	123	22 22	42	124	21 40	42	125	308
51	26 33	42	121	25 51	41	122	25 10	42	122	24 28	42	123	23 46	42	124	23 04	43	125	22 21	42	125	309
50	27 16	−42	121	26 34	−42	122	25 52	−42	123	25 10	−42	124	24 28	−43	125	23 45	−43	125	23 02	−43	126	310
49	27 58	42	122	27 16	42	123	26 34	42	124	25 52	43	125	25 09	43	125	24 26	43	126	23 43	44	127	311
48	28 41	43	123	27 58	42	124	27 16	43	125	26 33	43	125	25 50	44	126	25 06	43	127	24 23	44	128	312
47	29 23	43	124	28 40	43	125	27 57	43	125	27 14	44	126	26 30	44	127	25 46	44	128	25 02	44	128	313
46	30 04	43	125	29 21	43	125	28 38	44	126	27 54	44	127	27 10	44	128	26 26	44	129	25 42	45	129	314
45	30 46	−44	125	30 02	−44	126	29 18	−44	127	28 34	−44	128	27 50	−45	129	27 05	−45	129	26 20	−45	130	315
44	31 27	44	126	30 43	45	127	29 58	44	128	29 14	45	129	28 29	45	129	27 44	45	130	26 59	46	131	316
43	32 07	45	127	31 22	44	128	30 38	45	129	29 53	45	130	29 08	46	130	28 22	46	131	27 36	46	132	317
42	32 47	45	128	32 02	45	129	31 17	46	130	30 31	45	130	29 46	46	131	29 00	46	132	28 14	47	133	318
41	33 26	45	129	32 41	46	130	31 55	45	130	31 10	47	131	30 23	46	132	29 37	46	133	28 51	47	133	319
40	34 05	−46	130	33 19	−46	131	32 33	−46	131	31 47	−46	132	31 01	−47	133	30 14	−47	134	29 27	−47	134	320
39	34 44	47	131	33 57	46	132	33 11	47	132	32 24	47	133	31 37	47	134	30 50	47	134	30 03	48	135	321
38	35 21	46	132	34 35	47	132	33 48	47	133	33 01	48	134	32 13	47	135	31 26	48	135	30 38	48	136	322
37	35 59	47	133	35 12	48	133	34 24	47	134	33 37	48	135	32 49	48	136	32 01	49	136	31 12	48	137	323
36	36 36	48	134	35 48	48	134	35 00	48	135	34 12	48	136	33 24	49	137	32 35	48	137	31 47	49	138	324
35	37 12	−48	135	36 24	−49	135	35 35	−48	136	34 47	−49	137	33 58	−49	137	33 09	−49	138	32 20	−49	139	325
34	37 47	48	136	36 59	49	136	36 10	49	137	35 21	49	138	34 32	50	138	33 42	49	139	32 53	50	140	326
33	38 22	49	137	37 33	49	137	36 44	49	138	35 55	50	139	35 05	50	139	34 15	50	140	33 25	50	141	327
32	38 56	49	138	38 07	50	138	37 17	49	139	36 28	51	140	35 37	50	140	34 47	50	141	33 57	51	142	328
31	39 30	50	139	38 40	50	139	37 50	50	140	37 00	51	141	36 09	51	141	35 18	51	142	34 27	51	143	329
30	40 03	−50	140	39 13	−51	140	38 22	−51	141	37 31	−51	142	36 40	−51	142	35 49	−51	143	34 58	−52	144	330
29	40 35	51	141	39 44	51	142	38 53	51	142	38 02	51	143	37 11	52	144	36 19	52	144	35 27	52	145	331
28	41 07	52	142	40 15	51	143	39 24	52	143	38 32	52	144	37 40	52	145	36 48	52	145	35 56	53	146	332
27	41 37	51	143	40 46	52	144	39 54	53	144	39 01	52	145	38 09	53	146	37 16	52	146	36 24	53	147	333
26	42 07	52	144	41 15	53	145	40 22	52	146	39 30	53	146	38 37	53	147	37 44	53	147	36 51	54	148	334
25	42 36	−53	145	41 43	−52	146	40 51	−54	147	39 57	−53	147	39 04	−53	148	38 11	−54	148	37 17	−54	149	335
24	43 04	53	147	42 11	53	147	41 18	54	148	40 24	53	148	39 31	54	149	38 37	54	150	37 43	55	150	336
23	43 32	54	148	42 38	54	148	41 44	54	149	40 50	54	150	39 56	54	150	39 02	55	151	38 07	54	151	337
22	43 58	54	149	43 04	54	150	42 10	55	150	41 15	54	151	40 21	55	151	39 26	55	152	38 31	55	152	338
21	44 23	54	150	43 29	55	151	42 34	55	151	41 39	55	152	40 44	55	152	39 49	55	153	38 54	56	154	339
20	44 48	−55	152	43 53	−55	152	42 58	−55	153	42 03	−56	153	41 07	−55	154	40 12	−56	154	39 16	−56	155	340
19	45 12	56	153	44 16	55	153	43 21	56	154	42 25	56	154	41 29	56	155	40 33	56	155	39 37	56	156	341
18	45 34	56	154	44 38	56	155	43 42	56	155	42 46	56	156	41 50	56	156	40 54	57	157	39 57	56	157	342
17	45 56	57	155	44 59	56	156	44 03	57	156	43 06	56	157	42 10	57	157	41 13	57	158	40 16	56	158	343
16	46 16	57	157	45 19	56	157	44 23	57	158	43 26	57	158	42 29	57	159	41 32	57	159	40 35	57	159	344
15	46 35	−57	158	45 38	−57	159	44 41	−57	159	43 44	−57	159	42 47	−58	160	41 49	−57	160	40 52	−58	161	345
14	46 53	57	160	45 56	57	160	44 59	58	160	44 01	57	161	43 04	58	161	42 06	58	162	41 08	58	162	346
13	47 11	58	161	46 13	58	161	45 15	58	162	44 17	58	162	43 19	58	162	42 21	58	163	41 23	58	163	347
12	47 26	58	162	46 28	58	163	45 30	58	163	44 32	58	163	43 34	58	164	42 36	59	164	41 37	58	164	348
11	47 41	58	164	46 43	59	164	45 44	58	164	44 46	58	165	43 48	59	165	42 49	59	165	41 50	58	166	349
10	47 55	−59	165	46 56	−59	166	45 57	−58	166	44 59	−59	166	44 00	−59	166	43 01	−59	167	42 02	−58	167	350
9	48 07	59	167	47 08	59	167	46 09	59	167	45 10	59	167	44 11	59	168	43 12	59	168	42 13	59	168	351
8	48 18	59	168	47 19	59	168	46 20	59	169	45 21	60	169	44 21	59	169	43 22	59	169	42 23	59	170	352
7	48 28	60	170	47 28	59	170	46 29	59	170	45 30	60	170	44 30	59	170	43 31	59	171	42 32	60	171	353
6	48 36	59	171	47 37	60	171	46 37	59	171	45 38	60	172	44 38	59	172	43 39	60	172	42 39	59	172	354
5	48 44	−60	173	47 44	−60	173	46 44	−59	173	45 45	−60	173	44 45	−60	173	43 45	−59	173	42 46	−60	173	355
4	48 49	59	174	47 50	60	174	46 50	60	174	45 50	60	174	44 50	59	175	43 51	60	175	42 51	60	175	356
3	48 54	60	176	47 54	60	176	46 54	60	176	45 54	59	176	44 55	60	176	43 55	60	176	42 55	60	176	357
2	48 57	60	177	47 57	59	177	46 58	60	177	45 58	60	177	44 58	60	177	43 58	60	177	42 58	60	177	358
1	48 59	60	179	47 59	60	179	46 59	60	179	45 59	60	179	44 59	60	179	43 59	60	179	42 59	60	179	359
0	49 00	−60	180	48 00	−60	180	47 00	−60	180	46 00	−60	180	45 00	−60	180	44 00	−60	180	43 00	−60	180	360

S. Lat. {LHA greater than 180° ...... Zn=180−Z; LHA less than 180° ...... Zn=180+Z}

DECLINATION (0°-14°) CONTRARY NAME TO LATITUDE — LAT 33°

We must make a slight adjustment to H_c since we entered the table with only the degrees of the sun's declination and ignored the minutes and tenths. The small d is used with the minutes of declination to find this correction in the table on the last page of each volume of *H.O. 249*. Find the minutes of declination (round off the tenths) along the top and the d number on the side and take out the correction, giving it the sign that d had. This must be added to or subtracted from H_c.

Finally we compare the corrected computed height (H_c) we have gotten from the table with the observed height (H_o) we measured. The smaller is subtracted from the larger and the difference, called the *intercept*, is converted to nautical miles and labelled *toward* or *away*, to indicate whether our LOP is closer to the sun or farther from the sun than the AP. If H_o is greater than H_c, then it is toward, and vice versa.

Put away the books. The arithmetic is over and it is time to plot.

On our chart or plotting sheet we first plot the assumed position (see Figure 15-3). Its latitude will be the one we used to enter *H.O. 249*, and its longitude is the one we chose in finding LHA. We can refer back to our worksheet for these coordinates if necessary.

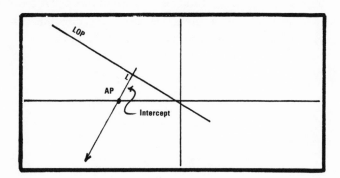

FIG. 15-3

We plot a line through the AP in the direction of Zn. This points toward the sun. It is good practice to put an arrowhead on it in the correct direction.

Along this line, starting from the AP, we measure off the length of the intercept in miles, either toward or away from the sun, and mark a point.

Finally, through that point we construct a perpendicular line, which is our LOP. It should be labeled as any other LOP with the time for which it was true, and the word SUN to indicate its source.

That is the process called reducing a sun sight by *H.O. 249*. It leaves us with a single LOP from a single timed observation of the sun. With some practice using the sextant and enough times through the tables and arithmetic so that careless errors are avoided, one can expect accuracy to better than a mile in the celestial LOP. That is more than adequate for a boat at sea, and good enough to be useful in many piloting situations as well. It will take many, many times through the process before it goes smoothly, and repetition is the *only* way to gain proficiency and confidence.

Appendix A summarizes all the steps once more for easy reference and to help remember what comes after what. It is quite possible to reduce a sight mechanically by simply following the steps, and for some that is the best way to procede. The *understanding* will come later. Others will find it useful to review the explanation of the process while working out sights, so that the reasons for each step are clear. The most important thing for a beginner is to get results, so pursue whatever approach works!

CHAPTER SIXTEEN

The Noon Sight

The procedure we have learned for reducing a sight of the sun at any time of the day by *H.O. 249* is by no means the only way an LOP can be obtained from a celestial reference point. The altitudes of other bodies (namely the stars, planets, and moon) can be measured and the LOP found by the same process. There are minor differences and peculiarities which will be discovered when the opportunity occurs to try these, and the necessary explanations will be found in the almanacs and tables.

One kind of sight is unique, however, and deserves special mention because it is so simple. The *noon sight* is one of the oldest of celestial observations, and mariners have used it for centuries to find their latitude from the sun because it is simple to understand and work out, requires no accurate knowledge of time, and is as precise as the device used to measure the sun's altitude. All that is required is a measurement of the sun's *highest altitude for the day* (which occurs at *local apparent noon*) and the sun's declination— either taken from the almanac or carefully estimated from knowledge of the date. From this information an LOP is found which lies exactly east-west and is therefore a line of latitude.

Prior to the invention of the chronometer in 1773, accurate time was not available to the navigator at sea, and ships had to depend largely on dead reckoning for their longitude. The noon sight provided accurate latitude, however, and common practice was to sail north or south to the latitude of the destination then stay on it until a landfall was made. The taking of the noon sight was a daily event of great importance, since to miss it meant waiting 24 hours for the next chance. Nowadays it is not of such critical importance, but it remains a standard part of the navigator's routine both from tradition and from the fact that it is quick and easy.

What makes it so simple is this: at one instant each day the sun and the boat are on the exact same meridian of longitude. This is the moment when the sun stops rising in the east and begins to set in the west, when it is no longer A.M. but becomes P.M. and is what we call local apparent noon (LAN). The sun will reach its highest point in the sky for the day and its bearing will be either true south or true north depending on the relative position of the observer. At this instant the triangle which we made out of the boat, the sun, and the north pole, collapses and becomes a straight line. We can easily diagram the situation in two dimensions by slicing the earth along this meridian as in Figure 16-1.

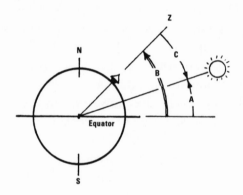

FIG. 16-1

The diagram shows three angles whose vertices are all at the earth's center and whose names we already know. Angle A is the sun's declination, angle B is the boat's latitude, and angle C is . . . our old friend zenith distance. Zenith distance—the angular distance between the sun and our zenith—is what we measure (indirectly) with the sextant. After reading H_s from the sextant and applying all the corrections to give us H_o, we subtract H_o from 90° and end up with zenith distance.

If we arrange to do this when the sun reaches its very highest point in the sky, we are then justified in drawing a diagram like Figure 16-1. On the diagram we can indicate the exact size of the zenith distance angle. Which other angle of the three do we know or can we find out? The sun's declination. We can go to the nautical almanac with the date and the time that we shot the sun and find the declination just as we did before. Because declination changes so slowly, the time does not have to be very exact, but now that we have easy access to accurate time we note the time of our sight the same as we would for any other sight. Do not forget to change it to GMT before entering the almanac!

If we show the size of the declination angle on our diagram, it should be immediately obvious that the third angle, latitude, can be found by simple arithmetic. In this case:

$$\text{Latitude} = \text{Zenith distance} + \text{Declination}$$

At different times of the year, and with the boat in different latitudes, the situation takes many forms, some of which are shown in Figure 16-2. The best way to know what to do is to draw the simple side-view diagram. Once the three angles are shown it will be easy to write the correct formula for latitude.

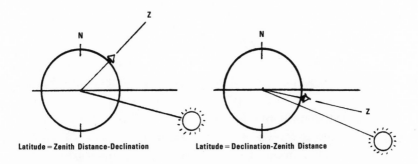

Latitude = Zenith Distance-Declination   Latitude = Declination-Zenith Distance

FIG. 16-2

There is only one other part of the noon sight process that needs consideration, and that is: How do we know when to be ready with our sextant to catch the sun at the moment it crosses our meridian?

Local apparent noon does not usually occur when our clocks read 12 noon. If we happen to be right at the center of our time zone it will occur close to 12 o'clock, but even then there are few times during the year when the sun is not either a bit ahead or a bit behind where it ideally should be.

A foolproof but time consuming method of finding LAN is to get on deck with a sextant quite early while the sun is still clearly rising, and begin measuring its altitude. Of course it will be increasing rapidly at first, but as LAN approaches, its rate of ascent will get slower and slower and finally stop. After a few minutes of no apparent change, it will begin to descend and we know that LAN has passed. But do not change the sextant reading when the sun begins to sink! We can then read from it the sun's highest altitude of the day.

To avoid the necessity of getting ready so far in advance, it is possible to predict what time local apparent noon will occur. The question really is at what time will the sun cross the longitude of the boat's DR? First we need to have an estimate of what the boat's longitude will be at noon, and this is simply done by projecting the intended course and speed from some fix or DR in the morning.

Next we look at the lower right-hand corner of the right-hand daily page of the almanac for our date. There we find under the heading "Mer. Pass." the times (GMT) at which the sun will cross the Greenwich meridian on each of the three days. We would like to know how much later it will be when the sun crosses *our* meridian. Since the sun travels west at a rate of 15° per hour we only have to convert the angle between us and Greenwich (our longitude) into time, and there is a table to make this quick and easy. The first yellow page in the almanac is called "Conversion of Arc to Time." If our DR longitude was 73° 34.2' we would first look up 73° and get four hours and 52 minutes, then look up 34' (accuracy greater than a minute is unnecessary) and get two minutes and 16 seconds. Together this means the sun will take four hours, 54 minutes, and 16 seconds to reach our longitude from Greenwich. Therefore, if LAN is at 11:57 at Greenwich, it will be at 16 51 16 (GMT) for us. Since we are in the fifth time zone our local time will be 11 51 16 at LAN. This arithmetic is summarized below:

Time of Meridian Passage from Almanac: GMT   11 57 00

DR longitude: 73 34.2 W
From Arc to Time Table: 73° → 4h 52m
                                    34' → + 2m 16s
                                  4h 54m 16s →   +4 54 16
GMT of LAN at long. 73 34 W: 16 51 16

Convert GMT to Zone Time: −5
Predicted Zone Time (local time) of LAN: 11 51 16

It should be kept in mind that this has been an *estimate* of when LAN will occur, so it is still necessary to be on deck a few minutes ahead of time to be sure not to miss the highest altitude.

The noonsight yields an LOP which happens to be the boat's latitude. On a typical day we will have shot the sun earlier in the morning when it was more nearly in the east and this would have given us an LOP running more or less north and south — or perhaps northeast-southwest. This earlier line would then be advanced according to our course and distance traveled during the morning, and crossed with the noon latitude for a running fix.

For a boat well at sea on an extended passage, a fix once a day at noon with careful dead reckoning in between can be all that is needed for keeping track of her progress. Of course, there will be days when the weather precludes taking sun sights and either we will trust our electronic instruments, or get by on dead reckoning for as long as we must. Closer to land, the need for more frequent fixes increases and we will be sure not to miss morning and evening twilight when both the horizon and the brighter stars are visible at the same time. When the altitudes of several stars are measured at nearly the same time, we are justified in calling the intersection of their resulting LOPs a fix. When three or more LOPs intersect at a point, we can be confident that we know where we are.

Electronic instruments are faster, easier, and often more accurate. But the navigator who understands how to use the celestial reference points will never have to live with the inescapable possibility that his instruments are lying to him. Few navigators are equipped to repair electronic instruments or to make any certain evaluation of whether or not they are working properly. In fact, a large part of the technology involved is being operated ashore or in orbit overhead and is therefore quite beyond his control. If something is wrong, how will he know? And even if he knows, what can be done?

The reliability of the sun, moon, stars, and planets, on the other hand . . .

APPENDIX A

Ten Easy Steps to Success with the Sun

1. Measure the sun's altitude with the sextant, and note the time.
2. Correct H_s to H_o, and express the time in GMT.
3. Enter the almanac with GMT. Find the sun's GHA and declination.
4. Pick an assumed latitude: nearest whole degree to your DR.
5. Pick an assumed longitude: nearest degree to your DR, but with minutes to match the minutes of GHA.
6. Combine assumed longitude and GHA to get LHA in whole degrees.
   For west longitude: LHA = GHA − long. (add 360 if necessary)
   For east longitude: LHA = GHA + long. (subtract 360 if necessary)
7. Enter *H.O. 249* with: a) Assumed latitude
   b) Declination (degrees only).
   Note *same* or *contrary* name.
   c) LHA
   Take out: H_c, Z, and *d*.
8. Enter table on back page with *d* and minutes of declina-

tion to get correction for H_c. Obey sign of d in applying correction to H_c.

9. Change Z to Zn. In north latitudes: Zn = Z
   for A.M. sights
   Zn = 360 − Z
   for P.M. sights

10. Compare H_c and H_o. Subtract the smaller from the larger to get intercept. One minute of angle = one nautical mile.
    If $H_o > H_c$, then label intercept Toward
    If $H_o < H_c$, then label intercept Away

TO PLOT:

1. Plot AP
2. Plot Zn through AP
3. Lay off intercept from AP, toward or away from the sun
4. Construct LOP through point thus found perpendicular to Zn.
5. Label it SUN with the local time.

APPENDIX B

Additional Readings

The following list of related readings is offered for those who wish to look further into the topics covered in this book.

Chapter 1 Freeman, Ira M. *Physics Made Simple*. Double-day & Co.
      Adkins, Jan. *Moving Heavy Things*. Walker & Co., NY.

Chapter 3 Marchaj, C.A. *Sailing Theory and Practice*. Dodd, Mead & Co.

Chapter 4 Adkins, Jan. *The Craft of Sail*. Walker & Co.

Chapter 5 Gill, P., Smith, J., Ziurys, E. *Internal Combustion Engines*. United States Naval Institute.

Chapter 6 Maloney, Elbert. *Chapman Piloting, Seamanship and Small Boat Handling*. Hearst Marine Books.
      Dunbar, B., Henderson, R. *Sail and Power*. United States Naval Institute.

Chapter 7 Jacobowitz, Henry. *Electricity Made Simple*. Doubleday & Co.

Chapters 8 to 16 Bowditch, Nathaniel. *The American Practical Navigator*. DMAHC.
      Mixter, George W. *Primer of Navigation*. Van Nostrand Reinhold Co.

Index